MW01114761

When I consider what some books have done for the world, and what they are doing, how they keep up our hope, awaken new courage and faith, soothe pain, give an ideal life to those whose hours are cold and hard, bind together distant ages and foreign lands, create new worlds of beauty, bring down the truth from heaven; I give eternal blessings for this gift, and thank God for books.

JAMES FREEMAN CLARKE

2/23/2012

Dear Mattie,
when you read this
beautiful book of inspirational
Poems and Stories, you
will remember the
numerous telephone calls,
love and friendship you
shared with a very
caring lady, your friend
Edna. Now, turn to
Page 221 to see a
beautiful smile I
love!
Blessings,
Always,
Drake

COPYRIGHT OF COMPILATION © 2010 BY WORKS OF WISDOM
Published and distributed in the United States by:
Works of Wisdom 406 Jay Street, Brooklyn New York 11201
Tel: (718) 797-3456.

Distributed in India by The Success Company, Mumbai.
Mona Thakkar Tel: 9920991814 email: jaisrikrsna0902@aol.com

Also available from: Pratham Ideas
#6 Guruprashad Bldg/Plot 192, Sion (East), Bombay 22.
Tel: 022-4035790 Cell: 989819202442

Book Production & Design:
America's Photoshop, New York. (718) 797-3456
Cover & Layout : Frenny Diaz - D1conceptz.com

HARD COVER EDITION
ISBN-10 0-9827539-1-8
ISBN-13 978-0-9827539-1-0

SOFT COVER EDITION
ISBN-10 0-9827539-2-6
ISBN-13 978-0-9827539-2-7

1ST EDITION, JULY 2010.

PRINTED IN KOREA.

Flowers 2
FROM MY GARDEN

Another bouquet of beautiful thoughts,
poems and stories

WORKS OF WISDOM
PUBLISHING

Please join me once again...

Mine has been the privilege to go back over many centuries of some of the finest written and spoken thoughts, poems and meditations. I have enjoyed picking for you the finest of what I have read over a lifetime, & once again presented it to you in this book.

Great philosophers of the ancient and modern times, teachers of virtue who showed a way of living the life sublime, poets who sang beautiful verses of love and human spirit, and many unrecognized and unremembered everyday people who left behind some priceless gem of inspiration, these are their words that we still have the good fortune to learn from.

There being too many overlapping subjects when one is to look to classify these inspirations and poems, I decided that my purpose should be for the reader to open the book at any page and find some word of the wise, an inspiring verse or an uplifting story which will enlighten in just a few minutes of reading. I call it the "feel better book".

A lot of the original sources are lost, or are now unknown, but thankfully the messages have endured. We still enjoy reading poems like the popular "Don't Quit" whose author is forgotten in time but the inspiration is still there.

Each and every one of us is here for a reason, and that we should be doing our best to fulfil our purpose on earth. This world inspite of its problems, is still a beautiful place to live in and there is goodness still found in the human heart.

Enjoy the book, and do write me your thoughts.

Until we meet again,

I remain, humbly yours

Yuvaraaj Thakkar
Spring 2010
New York.

For my mother and sister

Every day is a fresh beginning

Every morn is the world made new
You who are weary of sorrow and sinning,
Here is a beautiful hope for you.
A hope for me and a hope for you.

All the past things are past and over,
The tasks are done and the tears are shed.
Yesterday's errors let yesterday cover;
Yesterday's wounds which smarted and bled,
Are healed with the healing night has shed.

Everyday is a fresh beginning,
Listen, my soul to the glad refrain,
And spite of old sorrow and older sinning,
And puzzles forecasted, and possible pain,
Take heart with the day and begin again.

God works in mysterious ways.

Lately, we are going through some major changes on all fronts in our lives. People are loosing jobs in America due to the UPHEAVAL IN THE stock market and the re-structuring of many large companies, banks and other businesses. After having worked for years in a company, people are getting laid off without any pity as to what will be their condition when bills keep coming, children still needing things, healthcare and education burdens looming.

However, through all these challenges, there is always a ray of hope alive, waiting for us to roll up our sleeves and be ready for the Lord's blessings that we are about to receive. The following story is one such blessing as it makes us understand that through it all, there is always hope.

The only survivor of a shipwreck was washed up on a small, uninhabited island. He prayed feverishly for God to rescue him, and every day he scanned the horizon for help, but none seemed forthcoming.

Exhausted, he eventually managed to build a little hut out of driftwood to protect him from the elements and to store his few possessions. But then one day, after scavenging for food, he arrived home to find his little hut in flames, the smoke rolling up to the sky.

The worst had happened; everything was lost. He was stunned with grief and anger.

"God, how could you do this to me!" he cried.

Early the next day, however, he was awakened by the sound of a ship that was approaching the island. It had come to rescue him.

"How did you know I was here?" asked the weary man of his rescuers.

"We saw your smoke signal," they replied.

So, as you can see discouragement comes to us all, when the tide of life is low. But our faith should keep us believing that the good Lord is busily working in our life, even when things are not going our way.

Yuva

The Touch Of Hands

The hands of those I meet are dumbly eloquent to me. The touch of some hands is an impertinence. I have met people so empty of joy that when I grasp their frosty fingertips it seemed as I were shaking hands with a northeast storm. Others there are whose hands have sunbeams in them, so their grasp warms my heart.

It may be only the clinging touch of a child's hand, but there is as much potential sunshine in it for me as there is in a loving glance for others.

HELEN KELLER

People go into debt
trying to keep up with people who already are.

One sweetly solemn thought

Comes to me o'er and o'er;
I'm nearer my home today
Than I've ever been before;
Nearer my father's house,
Where the many mansions be;
Near the great white throne,
Nearer the jasper sea;
Nearer the bounds of life,
Where we lay our burdens down;
Nearer leaving the cross;
Nearer gaining the crown!

PHOEBE CARY

Dust if you must

But wouldn't it be better,
To paint a picture, or write a letter,
Bake a cake, or plant a seed?
Ponder the difference between want and need.
Dust if you must.
But there is not much time
With rivers to swim and mountains to climb!
Music to hear, and books to read,
Friends to cherish and life to lead.
Dust if you must.
But the world's out there
With the sun in your eyes,
the wind in your hair,
A flutter of snow, a shower of rain.
This day will not come round again.
Dust if you must.
But bear in mind,
Old age will come and it's not kind.
And when you go, and go you must,
You, yourself, will make more dust.

A grandmother and a little girl whose face was sprinkled with bright red freckles spent the day at the zoo.

The children were waiting in line to get their cheeks painted by a local artist who was decorating them with tiger paws. "You've got so many freckles, there's no place to paint!" a boy in the line cried.

Embarrassed, the little girl dropped her head. Her grandmother knelt down next to her. "I love your freckles," she said.

"Not me," the girl replied.

"Well, when I was a little girl I always wanted freckles" she said, tracing her finger across the child's cheek. "Freckles are beautiful!"

The girl looked up. "Really?"

"Of course," said the grandmother. "Why, just name me one thing that's prettier than freckles."

The little girl peered into the old woman's smiling face. "Wrinkles," she answered softly.

The answer is...

If you put a buzzard in a pen six or eight feet square and entirely open at the top, the bird, in spite of his ability to fly, will be an absolute prisoner. The reason is that a buzzard always begins a flight from the ground with a run of ten or twelve feet. Without space to run, as is his habit, he will not even attempt to fly, but will remain a prisoner for life in a small jail with no top.

The ordinary bat that flies around at night, a remarkable nimble creature in the air, cannot take off from a level place. If it is placed on the floor or flat ground, all it can do is shuffle about helplessly and, no doubt, painfully, until it reaches some slight elevation from which it can throw itself into the air. Then, at once, it takes off like a flash.

A Bumblebee if dropped into an open tumbler will be there until it dies, unless it is taken out. It never sees the means of escape at the top, but persists in trying to find some way out through the sides near the bottom. It will seek a way where none exists, until it completely destroys itself.

In many ways, there are lots of people like the buzzard, the bat and the bee. They are struggling about with all their problems and frustrations, not realizing that the answer is right there above them.

AT HEART AN OPTIMIST

This is a good world. We need not approve is all the items, nor of all the individuals in it; but the world itself is a friendly world. It has borne us; it has carried us onward; it has humanized us and guided our faltering footsteps throughout the long, slow advance; it has endowed us with strength and courage. It is full of tangle, of ups and downs. There is always enough to bite on, to sharpen wits on, to test our courage and manhood. It is indeed a world built for heroism, but also for beauty, tenderness, and mercy. I remain at the heart an optimist.

JAN CHRISTIAM SMUTS

The Love Of Books

When a man loves books he has in him that which will console him under many sorrows and strengthen him in various trails. Such a love will keep him at home, and make his time pass pleasantly. Even when visited by bodily or mental affliction he can resort to this book-love and be cured...... and when a man is at home and happy with a book, sitting by his fireside, he must be a churl if he does not communicate that happiness. Let him read now and then to his wife and children. Those thoughts will grow and take root in the hearts and minds of his listeners. A man who feels sympathy with what is good and noble, is at the time he feels that sympathy good and noble himself.

J. H. FRISWELL

The friend who just stands by

When trouble comes
your soul to try
You love the friend
who just "stands by"
Perhaps there's nothing
he can do
The thing is strictly
up to you;
For there are troubles
all your own,
And paths the soul
must tread alone;
Times when love
cannot smooth the road
Nor friendship lift
the heavy load,
But just to know
you have a friend
Who will "stand by"
until the end,
Whose sympathy
through all endures,
Whose warm handclasp
is always yours
It helps, someway,
to pull you through,
Although there's nothing
he can do.
And so with fervent heart
you cry,
"God bless the friend
who just "Stands by"!"

BERTYE YOUNG WILLIAMS

*If you feel far away
from God... Guess
who moved?*

*If You Want
Happiness*

If you want happiness
for an hour
Take a nap.
If you want happiness
for a day
Go fishing.
If you want happiness
for a month
Get married.
If you want happiness
for a year
Inherit a fortune.
If you want happiness
for a lifetime
Help someone else.

CHINESE PROVERB

A SURE HOPE

We speak too high
for things close by,
And lose what prayers
would find us;
For life has here
no charm so dear,
As home, sweet home,
and loved ones 'round us.

So long as there are
homes to which men turn
At close of day;
So long as there are homes
where children laugh,
And women stay;
If love and loyalty
and faith still hover
Across these sills,
a stricken nation will
sure recover
From all its gravest ills.

So long as there are
homes where fires burn,
And there is bread;
So long as there are
homes where lamps are lit,
And prayers are said;
Though people stumble
in the dark,
And nations grope,
With God at the helm
of every bark,
We have sure hope.

"Show me your God!"

the doubter cries.
I point him out the smiling skies;
I show him all the woodland greens;
I show him peaceful sylvan scenes;
I show him winter snows and frost;
I show him waters tempest-tossed;
I show him hills rock-ribbed and strong;
I bid him hear the thrush's song;
I show him flowers in the close
The lily, violet and rose;
I show him rivers, babbling streams;
I show youthful hopes and dreams;
I show him stars, the moon, the sun;
I show him deeds of kindness done;
I show him joy, I show him care,
And still he holds his doubting air,
And faithless goes his way, for he
Is blind of soul, and cannot see!

JOHN KENDRICK BANGS

It's really a wonder
that I haven't dropped all my ideals,
because they seem so absurd
and impossible to carry out.
Yet I keep them, because in spite of everything
I still believe that people are really good at heart.

ANNE FRANK

A woman and her friend are sitting together having lunch after one of the women's husband's funeral service. The friend asks the woman if her husband had any life insurance, and the widow answered her.

"Well, he had $10,000 in life insurance, but it is all gone."

"All gone?", the friend asks, shocked.

"Yes", said the widow.

"I don't understand", says the friend. "How did you already go through $10,000?"

Well, it is really not as bad as you think." says the widow. "I had to pay $5500 for his funeral and burial, $500 was donated to the church for the service, $1000 was what I spent on his suit, and $3000 was for the memorial stone."

Puzzled, the friend looks at the widow and says

"That must have been a huge stone for $3000!"

The widow answers: "Yeah, it was 3 carats!"

I SHALL NOT LIVE IN VAIN

If I can stop one heart from breaking

I shall not live in vain;

If I can ease one life aching,

Or cool one pain,

Or help one fainting robin

Into his nest again,

I shall not live in vain.

EMILY DICKINSON

Imagine a large circle and in the center of it rays of
light that spread out to the circumference. The light
in the center is God; each of us is a ray. The closer the
rays are to the center, the closer the rays are to one
another. The closer we live to God, the closer we are
bound to our neighbor.

The dreams ahead

What would we do in this world of ours
Were it not for the dreams ahead?
For thorns are mixed with the blooming flowers
No matter which path we tread.

And each of us has his golden goal,
Stretching far into the years;
And ever he climbs with a hopeful soul,
With alternate smiles and tears.

That dream ahead is what holds him up
Through the storms of a ceaseless fight;
When his lips are pressed to the wormwood's cups
And clouds shut out the light.

To some it's a dream of high estate;
To some it's a dream of wealth;
To some it's a dream of a truce with Fate
In a constant search for health.

To some it's a dream of home and wife;
To some it's a crown above;
The dreams ahead are what make each life –
The dreams – and faith -- and love!

A DAILY DOZEN

1. Believe in yourself, for you are marvelously endowed.
2. Believe in your job, for all honest work is sacred.
3. Believe in this day, for every minute contains an opportunity to do good.
4. Believe in your family, and create harmony by trust and co-operation.
5. Believe in your neighbor, for the more friends you can make, the happier you will be.
6. Believe in uprightness, for you cannot go wrong doing right.
7. Believe in your decisions; consult God first, then go ahead.
8. Believe in your health; stop taking your pulse, etc., etc.
9. Believe in your church; you encourage others to attend by attending yourself.
10. Believe in the now; yesterdays past recall and tomorrow may never come.
11. Believe in God's promises; He means it when He says, "I am with you always."
12. Believe in God's mercy; if God forgives you, you can forgive yourself – and try again tomorrow.

ALASTAIR MAC ODRUM

Take Time to Live

Take time to live;

The world has much to give,

Of faith and hope and love;

Of faith that life is good,

That human brotherhood

Shall no illusion prove;

Of hope that future years

Shall bring the best, in spite

Of those whose darkened sight

Would stir our doubts and fears;

Of love, that makes of life,

With all its grief's, a song;

A friend, of conquered wrong;

A symphony, of strife.

Take time to live,

Nor to vain mammon five

Your fruitful years.

Happiness adds and multiplies
as we divide it with others.

A NIELSEN

To be happy with a man, you must understand him a lot and love him a little.

To be happy with a woman, you must love her a lot and not try to understand her at all.

To give pleasure to a single heart by a single act is better than a thousand heads bowing in prayer.
MAHATMA GANDHI

Every strike brings me closer to the next home run.
GEORGE HERMAN RUTH

We've all got both light and dark inside us. What matters is the part we choose to act on. That's who we really are.
J.K. ROWLING

If you insist on perfection, make the first demand on yourself.

On Gratitude

Have you ever wondered what power lies in ten minutes?
In a world of emails, and cell phones and the hustle bustle of life, we have taken so much for granted. Like relationships and friendships.
If you feel that there is someone whose life has impacted yours in a happy positive way, and you have been enriched by their association, pick up a piece of paper and write them how truly grateful you are. That person will be happier, and so will you. In just ten minutes that will take to write a letter, you have made two people happy.
I teach my children that Gratitude is the first quality one must develop. It works wonders. Happiness is a result of being grateful for the blessings in our lives, be it in friendships, or relationships. There are many reasons to be grateful:

> For the gift of life
> For the warmth of friendships
> For good health and a cheerful disposition
> For the loving and caring we receive
> For the treasures of books
> For the gift of having a family
> For the enjoyment of good poetry and music
> For the colors of mother nature
> For the satisfaction of work
> For the abundance of God's blessings.

The list can be endless when you really think of it. So next time you choose to be happy, take the path of gratitude. You will see how easy it is to be joyful.

Yuwa

Some people think its holding on that makes one strong. Sometimes it's letting go.
SYLVIA ROBINSON

A true friend never gets in your way unless you happen to be going down.
ANDREW GLASOW

Recall it as often as you wish, a happy memory never wears out.
LIBBIE FUDIM

If you can carry your childhood with you, you never become older.
A SUTZKEVER

Love is a friendship set to music.
E. JOSEPH COSSMAN

There are times when silence has the loudest voice.
LEROY BROWNLOW

The best and most beautiful things in the world cannot be seen or even touched. they must be felt with the heart.
HELEN KELLER

A little fellow follows me

A careful man I ought to be,
A little fellow follows me,
I do not dare to go astray
For fear he'll go the selfsame way.

Not once can I escape his eyes;
Whate'er he sees me do he tries.
Like me says he's going to be
That little chap who follows me.

He thinks that I am good and fine;
Believe in every word of mine.
The base in me he must not see
That little chap who follows me.

I must remember as I go,
Thro' summer sun and winter snow,
I'm building for the years to be
That little chap who follows me.

Where there is no vision
a people perish.
EMERSON

Goodness
never goes wasted.
YUVA

*God give me joy in
the common things*

In the dawn that lures, the eve that
stings.

In the new grass sparking after rain,
In the late wind's wild and weird re-
frain;

In the springtime's spacious field of
gold,
In the precious light by winter doled.

God give me joy in the love of friends,
In their dear home talk as summer
ends;

In the songs of the children, unre-
strained;
In the sober wisdome age as gained.

God give me joy in the tasks that press,
In the memories that burn and bless;

In the thought that life has love to
spend,
In the faith that God's at journey's end.

God give me hope for each day tha
springs,
God give me joy in the common
things!

THOMAS CURTIS CLARK

The fragrance
of what you give away
stays with you.
EARL ALLEN

You can't be envious
and happy for some-
one at the same time.
LOPE DE VEGA

The shifts of fortune
test the reliability of
friends.
CICERO

Pardon, not wrath, is
God's best attribute.
B. TAYLOR

The company
makes the feast.
PROVERB

Ask God
for a thankful heart.
GEORGE HERBERT

Those things that hurt
instruct.
B. FRANKLIN

Speak Gently

Speak gently, it is better far
To rule by love than fear;
Speak gently, let no harsh word mar
The good we may do here.

Speak gently to the little child;
Its love be sure to gain;
Teach it in accents soft and mild;
It may not long remain.

Speak gently to the young; for they
Will have enough to bear;
Pass through this life as best they May,
'Tis full of anxious care.

Speak gently to the aged one.
Grieve not the care worn heart;
Whose sands of life are nearly run,
Let such in peace depart.

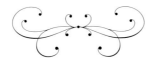

A young man packing his bag for a journey said to a friend, "I have nearly finished packing. All I have to put in are:

> A guidebook,
>
> A lamp,
>
> A mirror,
>
> A microscope,
>
> A telescope,
>
> A volume of fine poetry,
>
> A few biographies,
>
> A package of old letters,
>
> A book of songs,
>
> A sword,
>
> A hammer, and
>
> A set of tools."

"But you cannot put all that into your bag," objected the friend. "Oh, yes," said he. "Here it is." And he placed his Bible in the corner of the suitcase and closed the lid.

When I meditated on the word Guidance,
kept seeing "dance" at the end of the word.
While reading, I began thinking that God's will
is a lot like dancing.
When two people try to lead, nothing feels right.
The movement doesn't flow with the music,
and everything is quite uncomfortable and jerky.

When one person realizes that, and lets the other lead,
both bodies begin to flow with the music.
One gives gentle cues, perhaps with a nudge to the back
or by pressing Lightly in one direction or another.

It's as if two become one body, moving beautifully.
The dance takes surrender, willingness,
and attentiveness from one person
and gentle guidance and skill from the other.

My eyes drew back to the word Guidance.

When I saw "G: I thought of God, followed by "u" and "i".
"God, "u" and "i" "dance."
God, you, and I dance.
As I lowered my head, I became willing to trust
that I would get guidance about my life.
Once again, I became willing to let God lead.
My prayer for you today is that God's blessings
and mercies be upon you on this day and everyday.

May you abide in God as God abides in you.

Dance together with God, trusting God to lead
and to guide you through each season of your life.
This prayer is powerful and there is nothing attached.
If God has done anything for you in your life,

Truly, prayer is one of the best gifts we can receive.
There is no cost but a lot of rewards;
so let's continue to pray for one another.

And I Hope You Dance

IN MEMORIAM

DOWNEY

EDNA MAY FARQUHARSON DOWNEY
"Auntie"
November 13, 1921 ~ May 17, 2010

Dearest Mommy,
Everyday we continue to share your wonderful
life of love, friendship and kindness with family
and friends. We all miss you so very much!
Your daughter and best friend, Diane,
Family and Friends

62° at 2:00 p.m.	62° at 3:00 p.m.
29° at 6:53 a.m.	31° at 3:42 a.m.
59°/36°	58°/38°
74° in 1964	78° in 1879
22° in 1973	18° in 1957
None	None
0.07"	0.12"
1.35"	1.30"
39.63"	49.69"
36.52"	36.51"
81% at 7 a.m.	75% at 3 a.m.
30% at 2 p.m.	30% at 3 p.m.
30.15"	30.15"
30.08"	30.08"

nd forecast ▮ Normal • Record

Wind Chill:
27°
(Comfort index combines temperature and wind.)

You are strong . . . .
when you take your grief and teach it to smile.

You are brave . . . .
when you overcome your fear and help others to do the same.

You are happy . . . .
when you see a flower and give it your blessing.

You are loving . . . .
when your own pain does not blind you to the pain of others.

You are wise . . . .
when you know the limits of your wisdom.

You are true . . . .
when you admit there are times you fool yourself.

You are alive . . . .
when tomorrow's hope means more to you than yesterday's mistake.

You are growing . . . .
when you know what you are but not what you will become.

You are free . . . .
when you are in control of yourself and do not wish to control others.

You are honorable . . . .
when you find your honor is to honor others.

You are generous . . . .
when you can take as sweetly as you can give.

You are humble . . . .
when you do not know how humble you are.

You are thoughtful . . . .
when you see me just as I am and treat me just as you are.

You are merciful . . . .
when you forgive in others the faults you condemn in yourself.

You are beautiful . . . .
when you don't need a mirror to tell you.

You are rich . . . .
when you never need more than what you have.

You are you . . . .
when you are at peace with who you are not.

My Philosophy

To live as gently as I can;
To be, no matter where, a man;
To take what comes of good or ill
And cling to faith and honor still;
To do my best, and let that stand
The record of my brain and hand;
And then, should failure come to me,
Still work and hope for victory.

To have no secret place wherein
I stoop unseen to shame or sin;
To be the same when I'm alone
And when my every deed is known;
To live undaunted, unafraid
Of any step that I have made;
To be without pretense or sham
Exactly what men think I am.

To leave some simple mark behind
To keep my having lived in mind;
If enmity to aught I show.
To be an honest, generous foe,
To play my little part, nor whine
That greater honors are not mine.
This, I believe, is all I need
For my philosophy and creed.

EDGAR A. GUEST

*I am always content
with what happens
for I know that what God chooses
is better than what I choose.*

EPICTETUS

People are often unreasonable, irrational, and self centered. Forgive them anyway.
If you are kind, people may accuse you of selfish, ulterior motives. Be kind anyway.
If you are successful, you will win some unfaithful friends and some genuine enemies. Succeed anyway.
If you are honest and sincere, people my deceive you. Be honest and sincere anyway.
What you spend years creating, others could destroy overnight. Create anyway.
If you find serenity and happiness, some may be jealeous. Be happy anyway.
The good you do today, will often be forgotten. Do good anyway.
Give the best you have, and it will never be enough. Give you best anyway.
In final analysis, it is between you and God. It was never between you and them anyway.

KENT KEITH

Oh Gosh," sighed the wife one morning, "I'm convinced my mind is almost completely gone!"

Her husband looked up from the newspaper and commented, "I'm not surprised: You've been giving me a piece of it every day for twenty years!"

Isn't it amazing how soon later comes after you buy now.

What's meant to be will always find a way.
TRISHA YEARWOOD

It's not the load that breaks you down, it's the way you carry it.
LOU HOLTZ

A bird doesn't sing because it has an answer, it sings because it has a song.
MAYA ANGELOU

There is neither happiness nor unhappiness in this world; there is only the comparison of one state with another. Only a man who has felt ultimate despair is capable of feeling ultimate bliss. It is necessary to have wished for death in order to know how good it is to live.....the sum of all human wisdom will be contained in these two words: Wait and Hope.

ALEXANDRE DUMAS
THE COUNT OF MONTE CRISTO

All the darkness in the world can't extinguish the light from a single candle.
FRANCIS OF ASSISI

Those who say the least often say the most.

Be Hopeful

Be hopeful, friend, when clouds are dark and days are gloomy, dreary,
Be hopeful even when the heart is sick and sad and weary.
Be hopeful when it seems your plans are all opposed and thwarted;
Go not upon life's battlefield despondent and fainthearted.

And, friends, be hopeful of yourself. Do bygone follies haunt you?
Forget them and begin afresh. And let no hindrance haunt you.
Though unimportant your career may seem as you begin it,
Press on, for victory's ahead. Be hopeful, friend, and win it.

STRICKLAND GILLIAN

Ua ola loko i ke aloha

which means...
Love Gives Life Within"

HAWAIIAN

If your actions
inspire others to
dream more
learn more
do more
become
then you are a leader.

JOHN QUINCY ADAMS

A Little Word

A little word of kindness spoken,
A motion or a tear,
Has often healed the heart that's broken!
And made a friend sincere.

A word – a look – has crushed to earth,
Full many a budding flower,
Which had a smile but owned its birth,
Would bless life's darkest hour.

Then deem it not an idle thing,
A pleasant word to speak;
The face you wear, the thoughts you bring, a heart may heal or break.

It isn't the money you are making,
It isn't the clothes you wear;
It isn't the skill of your good right hand
That makes folks really care.
But it's the smile on your face
And the light of your eyes,
And the burdens that you bear;
It's how do you live, and neighbor,
It's how do you work and play,
And it's how do you say, "Good Morning"
To the people along the wayl
And it's how do you face your troubles
Whenever the skies are gray.

BYRNE

An Illinois man left the snow-filled streets of Chicago for a vacation in Florida. His wife was on a business trip and was planning to meet him there the next day. When he reached his hotel, he decided to send his wife a quick email.

Unfortunately, when typing her address, he missed one letter, and his note was directed instead to an elderly preacher's wife whose husband had passed away only the day before. When the grieving widow checked her email, she took one look at the monitor, let out a piercing scream, and fell to the floor in a dead faint.

At the sound, her family rushed into the room and saw this note on the screen:

Dearest Wife,
Just got checked in. Everything prepared for your arrival tomorrow.
P.S. Sure is hot down here.

As long as you have life and breath, believe. Believe for those who cannot. Believe even if you have stopped believing. Believe for the sake of the dead, for love, to keep your heart beating, believe. Never give up, never despair, let no mystery confound you into the conclusion that mystery cannot be yours.

MARK HELPRIN

Once you learn to quit, it becomes a habit.

VINCE LOMBARDI.

It's the magic of risking everything for a dream that nobody sees but you.

MILLION DOLLAR BABY

Believe there is a great power silently working all things for good, behave yourself and never mind the rest.

BEATRIX POTTER

To be in your children's memories tomorrow, You have to be in their lives today.

BARBARA JOHNSON

Having it all, for nothing

Mahatma Gandhi, the social reformer of India, and one of its greatest souls said contentment was the key to happier living. He was a lawyer who could have easily made lots of money for himself, but life thrusted in his lap, the responsibility of awakening the people to the idea of a free India, free from British tyranny.

Contentment does not mean not wanting more, it simply means being happy with what we have. The greedy person is always looking at other people's dinner plates rather than enjoy what's in their own. Enjoy your blessings, of which many have few.

To find real contentment and to live well requires that you examine yourself and find what it is that makes you happy.

I read a story of a lottery winner a couple of years ago, who won millions of dollars but is now living on just a few hundred dollars a month in government hand-out and food stamps. He had won a $16 million lotto! The reason he lost it all, is simple. He did not know how to manage what life had blessed him with.

A peace of mind, a clear conscience, a positive attitude towards life, kindness towards the problems of others, a spirit of happiness and gratitude, these are your real riches along with the magic of contentment.

Material possessions make us want more. Five million dollars in the bank and we are chasing the sixth, and the seventh, and.....

No one can say he or she can eat one piece of hot French fries. We want more. It's the same with money and material possessions. They possess us, and unless we learn to tame ourselves, we will be forever craving. Making lots of money is not wrong, not knowing what to do with the extra to help others is.

A well known movie producer, who was also an aviator died a few years ago. At his funeral, a lady in attendance was asked by an inquisitive reporter, "How much did Howie leave?" and she replied, "He left it all".

One of my favorite singers of Indian cinema passed away. a few years back. All her estate was fought over by the undeserving and the government. She had a chance to leave it to good charities, but she held on to it all. What a waste. Don't let your blessings go wasted. Give while you can, because it's already later for some people than you think.

Yuva

Attitudes

When you extend pure love
to everyone with selfless motivation
that is an attitude of kindness.
When you send good wishes and pure feelings
to those who are in deep sorrow,
that is an attitude of mercy.
When you see the virtues
rather than the weaknesses in people
that is an attitude of compassion.
When you bless and uplift someone
even as they defame you,
that is an attitude of forgiveness.
When you tolerate a situation and
take responsibility as well as give cooperation
even when not appreciated
that is an attitude of humility and self-respect.
Every second, every moment and
every breath of your life is nurtured by attitude.

He leadeth Me

In pastures green?
Not always; sometimes He
Who knoweth best, in kindness leadeth me
In many ways where heavy shadows be.
Out of the sunshine
warm and soft and bright –
Out of the sunshine into the darkest night,
I oft would faint with sorrow and affright,
Only for this – I know He holds my hand;
So whether in the green or desert land
I trust although I may not understand.

And by still waters? No, not always so;
Ofttimes the heavy tempests
round me blow,
And o'er my soul the waters and billows go.
But when the storms beat loudest and I cry
Aloud for help, the Master standeth by
And whispers to my soul, "Lo, it is I."
Above the tempest wild I hear Him say,
"Beyond this darkness lies a perfect day.
In every path of thine I lead the way."
So whether on the hilltops high and fair
I dwell, or in the sunless valleys where
The shadows lie – what matters? He is there.
So where He leads me, I can safely go,
And in the blest hereafter I shall know
Why, in His wisdom, He hath led me so.

REV. JOHN F. CHAPLAIN

The most difficult advice
in the world to follow is
that which you give
to others.

A coincidence
is a small miracle
where God chose to
remain anonymous.

A day hemmed in prayer
is less likely to unravel.

Of all the things you wear,
your expression
is the most important.

Respect is what we owe;
love is what we give.

The mystery of love is
that the more you give,
the more remains
in your heart.

A friend is one
who comes in,
when the whole world
has gone out.

If you see someone
without a smile,
give him one of yours.

Luck is where opportunity
meets preparation.

A smile always adds to
your face value.

Experience
is what you get,
when you didn't get
what you wanted.

May you always have

Enough happiness to keep you sweet;
Enough trials to keep you strong;
Enough sorrow to keep you human;
Enough hope to keep you happy;
Enough failure to keep you humble;
Enough success to keep you eager;
Enough friends to give you comfort;
Enough faith in yourself to give you courage;
Enough wealth to meet your needs; and
Enough determination to make each day a good day.

When money talks, people hardly pay attention to the grammar.

Recently in a booklet on the subject of a middle age, a prominent authority pointed out that it is a dangerous age and recommended ten substitutes for middle-age diversions:

1. One less hour of worry – for one more hour of laughter.
2. One less week of high-pressure living – for one more week o restful vacation.
3. One less luncheon conference – for one more midday period of relaxation.
4. One less evening of formal society – for one more evening with a jolly book.
5. One less elaborate banquet – for one more quite supper with the family.
6. One less hour under the electric light – for one more in the sunshine.
7. One less hour in the automobile – for one more swinging along on foot.
8. One less hour of work – for one more physical examination by my doctor.
9. One less pound of flabby body fat – for one more of tougher muscle.
10. One less helping of sweets – for one more of vegetables.

A woman's work is never done, especially if she depends on her husband or the kids to do it.

Langston Hughes says: Hold fast to dreams, for if dreams die, life is a broken-winged bird that cannot fly.

Light tomorrow with today.
ELIZABETH BARRETT BROWNING

The great painter believed that great things are not accidental, but most certainly willed.

Nothing makes a marriage rust like distrust.

Vocabulary of Values

Five most important words
I am proud of you.
Four most important words
What is your opinion?
Three most important words
If you please.
Two most important words
thank you.
Least most important word

I.

The wheel was one of man's greatest inventions until he got behind it.

If you want to be liked
keep your ears open
and most of the time
keep your mouth shut.

When everything
goes dead wrong
look and see
if you are not facing
the wrong direction.

You Prayed for Me

You did not know my need,
Or that my heart was sore indeed,
Or that I had a fear I could not quell
You sensed that with me
all was not quite well,
And so – you prayed for me.

My path had seemed so black,
And yet I know there was no turning back,
Then in my loneliness I felt God near,
And down the long dark road
a light showed clear.
Because – you prayed for me.
And as your prayer,
like incense sweet did soar.

God did love,
on me a blessing pour,
The day – you prayed for me.

My father and me

Most of us go through growing pains and the generation gap syndrome. I was a rebel in my teenage years and was always on the wrong side of things with my father. Thirty years later, I have come to realize what an amazing man he is, and when I read this in an old magazine, I could relate to it very well because now I have my own kids and everything my father said feels like golden words that could have helped me in my youth. Well, its never too late to learn.

When I was 4 Yrs Old : My father is THE BEST.
When I was 6 Yrs Old : My father seems to know everyone.
When I was 10 Yrs Old : My father is excellent but he is short tempered.
When I was 12 Yrs Old : My father was nice when I was little.
When I was 14 Yrs Old : My father started being too sensitive.
When I was 16 Yrs Old : My father can't keep up with modern time.
When I was 18 Yrs Old : My father is getting less tolerant as the days pass by.
When I was 20 Yrs Old : It is too hard to forgive my father, how could my mother stand him all these years.
When I was 25 Yrs Old : My father seems to be objecting to everything I do.
When I was 30 Yrs Old: It's very difficult to be in agreement with my father, I wonder if my Grandfather was troubled by my father when he was a youth.
When I was 40 Yrs Old: My father brought me up with a lot of discipline, I must do the same.
When I was 45 Yrs Old: I am puzzled, how did my father manage to raise all of us.
When I was 50 Yrs Old : It's rather difficult to control my kids, how much did my father suffer for the sake of upbringing and protecting us.
When I was 55 Yrs Old: My father was far looking and had wide plans for us, he was gentle and outstanding.
When I became 60 Yrs Old: My father is THE BEST.

Note that it took 56 Yrs to complete the cycle and return to the starting point My father is THE BEST.

Let's be good to our parents before it's too late and pray to God that our own children will treat us even better than the way we treated our parents.

$\mathcal{I}$ watched intently as my little brother was caught in the act. He sat in the corner of the living room, a pen in one hand and my father's brand-new hymnbook in the other.

As my father walked into the room, my brother cowered slightly; he sensed that he had done something wrong. From a distance I could see that he had opened my father's new hymnal and scribbled in it the length and breadth of the first page with a pen. Now, staring at my father fearfully, he and I both waited for his punishment. And as we waited, there was no way we could have known that our father was about to teach us deep and lasting lessons about life and family, lessons that continue to become even clearer through the years.

My father picked up his prized hymnal, looked at it carefully, and then sat down, without saying a word. Books were precious to him; he was a clergyman and the holder of several degrees. For him, books were knowledge, and yet he loved his children. What he did next was remarkable. Instead of punishing my brother, instead of scolding or yelling or reprimanding, he sat down, took the pen from my brother's hand, and then wrote in the book himself, alongside the scribbles John had made: John's work, 1959, age 2. How many times have I looked into your beautiful face and into your warm, alert eyes looking up at me and thanked God for the one who has now scribbled in my new hymnal. You have made the book sacred, as have your brothers and sister to so much of my life.

"Wow," I thought. "This is punishment?"

A lesson in Love

The years and the books came and went. Our family experienced what all families go through and perhaps a little bit more: triumph and tragedy, prosperity and loss, laughter and tears. We gained grandchildren but we lost a son. We always knew our parents loved us and that one of the proofs of their love was the hymnal by the piano. From time to time we would open it, look at the scribbles, read my father's expression of love, and feel uplifted.

Now I know that through this simple act my father taught us how every event in life has a positive side - if we are prepared to look at it from another angle — we see how precious it is when our lives are touched by little hands. But he also taught us about what really matters in life: people, not objects; tolerance, not judgment; love, not anger. Now I, too, am a father, and, like my dad, a clergyman and holder of degrees. But unlike my father, I do not wait for my daughters to secretly take books from my bookshelf and scribble in them. From time to time I take one down - not just a cheap paperback, but a book that I know I will have for many years to come, and I give it to one of my children to scribble or write their names in. And as I look at their artwork, I think about my father, the lessons he taught me, the love he has for us, and which I have for my children - love that is at the very heart of a family.

I think about these things and I smile. Then I whisper, "Thank you, Dad."

ARTHUR BOWLER

When you are inspired be some great purpose, some extraordinary project, all your thoughts break their bonds;

Your mind transcends limitations, your consciousness expands in every direction, and you find yourself in a new, great and wonderful world.

Dormant forces, faculties and talents become alive, and you discover yourself to be a greater person by far than you ever dreamed yourself to be.

PATANJALI

Whatever is-is best

That each sorrow has its purpose,
By the sorrowing oft unguessed,
But as sure as the sun brings morning,
Whatever is-is best.

I know that each sinful action,
As sure as the night brings shade;
Is somewhere, sometime punished,
Tho' be long delayed;

I know that the soul is aided
Sometimes by the heart's unrest,
And to grow means often to suffer—
But whatever is-is best.

I know there are no errors
In the great Eternal plan
And all things work together
For the final good of man;

And I know when my soul speeds onward
In its grand, eternal quest,
I shall say as I look back earthward,
Whatever is-is best.

ALEXANDER POPE IN "ESSAY ON MAN"

It's important to believe in yourself. Believe that you can do it under any circumstances. Because if you believe you can, Then you really will. That belief just keeps you searching for answers, and then pretty soon you get it.

WALLY "FAMOUS" AMOS

He who has lost his confidence can lose nothing more.

BOISTE

Self love, my dear, is not so vile a sin as self neglect.

WILLIAM SHAKESPEARE

A vacation is a holiday
from everything
except expenses.

*There is just no justice.
If you fill your
income tax correctly,
you go to the poorhouse.
If you don't, you go to jail.*

"Those who make us believe that anything's possible and fire our imagination over the long haul, are often the ones who have survived the bleakest of circumstances. The men and women who have every reason to despair, but don't, may have the most to teach us, not only about how to hold true to our beliefs, but about how such a life can bring about seemingly impossible social change. "

PAUL ROGAT LOEB

Only as high as I reach can I grow
Only as far as I seek can I go
Only as deep as I look can I see
Only as much as I dream can I be.

Brothers All

We're brothers all, whatever the place,
Brothers whether in rags or lace,
Brothers all, but the good Lord's grace.

Some may sit in a royal hall,
Some may dwell where the rooms are small,
But under the skin we are brothers all.

Some may toil 'neath the burning sun,
Some may dream where the waters run,
But we're brothers all when the day is done.

By the sun that shines and the rains that fall,
By the shadows flung on the garden wall,
By the good Lord's grace, we are brothers all.

By the hurt that comes and the falling tear,
By the common grief at the silent bier,
And the grave that awaits, we are brothers
here.

EDGAR A. GUEST

If we pray, we will believe;
if we believe, we will love;
if we love, we will serve.

MOTHER THERESA

A man attending church
regularly
is not the same as attending
religiously.

when you think about it...

Gossip is ear pollution.

In the present condition, if someone offers you the world on a silver platter, take the platter.

At Christmas, most parents spend more money on their children than they did on the honeymoon vacation that started it all.

The best thing for gray hair is a sensible head underneath.

Its pretty hard to make a name for yourself in the sun if you keep resting in the shade of the family tree.

A good education enables a person to worry about things ignorant people don't know exists.

Some folks aren't interested in anything unless its none of their business.

By the time a man reaches greener pastures, he is out of breath to climb over the fence.

Knowledge is knowing a fact. Wisdom is knowing what to do with that fact.

"I've learned that people will forget what you said, people will forget what you did, but people will never forget how you made them feel."

MAYA ANGELOU

"The man who does not read good books has no advantage over the man who can't read them."

MARK TWAIN

"We are all in the gutter, but some of us are looking at the stars."

OSCAR WILDE

You don't attract what you want, you attract what you are.

When there is a lot of it around, you never seem to want it very much.

Kind words do not cost much. They never blister the tongue or lips. They make other people good-natured. They also produce their own image on men's souls, and a beautiful image it is.

BLAISE PASCAL

Love is the very essence of life. It is the pot of gold at the end of the rainbow. Yet it is not found only at the end of the rainbow. Love is at the beginning also, and from it springs the beauty that arched across the sky on a stormy day. Love is the security for which children weep, the yearning of youth, the adhesive that binds marriage, and the lubricant that prevents devastating friction in the home; it is the peace of old age, the sunlight of hope shining through death. How rich are those who enjoy it in their associations with family, friends, and neighbors! Love, like faith, is a gift of God. It is also the most enduring and most powerful virtue.

GORDON B. HINCKLEY

Laugh a little Love a little

As you go your way!
Work a little – play a little,
Do this every day!

Give a little – take a little,
Never mind a frown
Make your smile a welcomed thing
All around the town!

Laugh a little – love a little
Skies are always blue!
Every cloud has silver linings
But it's up to you!

PHILLIPS

"This is what you shall do; Love the earth and sun and the animals, despise riches, give alms to every one that asks, stand up for the stupid and crazy, devote your income and labor to others, hate tyrants, argue not concerning God, have patience and indulgence toward the people, take off your hat to nothing known or unknown or to any man or number of men, go freely with powerful uneducated persons and with the young and with the mothers of families, read these leaves in the open air every season of every year of your life, re-examine all you have been told at school or church or in any book, dismiss whatever insults your own soul, and your very flesh shall be a great poem and have the richest fluency not only in its words but in the silent lines of its lips and face and between the lashes of your eyes and in every motion and joint of your body."

WALT WHITMAN

Remember, amateurs built the ark.
Professionals built the Titanic.

There can be no happiness if the things we
believe in are different from the things we do.
FREYA STARK

The only people we can't forgive are the ones
we are still afraid of.
GRAMMA MILDRED

Every day, tell at least one person something you
like, admire, or appreciate about them.
RICHARD CARLSON

The vision that you glorify in your mind,
the ideal that you enthrone
in your heart, this you will
build your life by,
and this you will become.
JAMES ALLEN

Thanks

For sunlit hours and visions clear,
For all remembered faces dear.
For comrades of a single day
Who sent us stronger on our way,
For friends who shared the year's long road
And bore with us the common load,
For hours that levied heavy tolls
But brought us nearer to our goals,
For insights won through toil and tears,
We thank the Keeper of the Years.
CLYDE MCGEE

First Impressions

It is not tight to judge a man
by hasty glance or passing whim,
Or think that first impressions can
tell all there is to know of him.

Who knows what weight of weariness
the man we rashly judge may bear,
The burden of his loneliness,
his blighted hopes, his secret care.
A pompous guise or air of pride
may only be an outward screen,
A compensation meant to hide
a baffled will, a grief unseen.

However odd a person seems,
however strange his ways may be,
Within each human spirit gleams
a spark of true divinity.

So what can first impressions tell?
Unthinking judgments will not do,
Who really knows a person well
may also come to like him too!

ALFRED GRANT WALTON

Into my heart's treasury
I slipped a coin
That time cannot take
Nor a thief purloin,
Oh better than the minting
of a gold-crowned king
Is the safe-kept memory
Of a lovely thing.

SARA TEASDALE

You'll always stay young if

you live honestly
eat slowly
sleep sufficiently
worship faithfully
and lie about your age.

All some of us learn from
our mistakes is to
blame them on others.

When a horse is broke
he is tame,
When a man is broke
he gets wild.

You can battle to the top
or bottle to the bottom.

What most people are
looking for, is a blessing
not in disguise.

The ships that come in
while we sit and wait
are mostly hardships.

Most of the time it is
thinking about the load
that makes you tired.

It takes a child about two
years to learn to talk and
a man fifty years to keep
his mouth shut.

A prayer in its simplest definition

....is merely a wish turned Godward.

PHILLIP BROOKS

The Art of Hope

The well-known maxim, "While there is life there is hope," has deeper meaning in reverse: "Where there is hope there is life."

Hope comes first, life follows. Hope gives power to life. Hope rouses life to continue, to expand, to grow, to reach out, to go on.

Hope sees a light where there isn't any.

Hope lights candles in millions of despairing hearts.

Hope is the miracle medicine of the mind. It inspires the will to live.

Hope is physician's strongest ally.

Hope is man's shield and buckler against defeat.

"Hope," wrote Alexander Pope, "springs eternal in the human breast." And as long as it does man will triumph and move forward.

Hope never sounds retreat. Hope keeps the banners flying.

Hope revives ideals, renew dreams, visions.

Hopes scales the peak, wrestle with the impossible, achieves the highest aim.

"The word which God has written on the brow of every man," wrote Victor Hugo, "is Hope." As long as man has hope no situation is hopeless.

WILFERD A. PETERSON

Wilferd Peterson wrote some of the best self help books I read as a teenager while. He was kind enough to share his writings with me, and give me permission to share them with others. He lived in Grand Rapids, Michigan.

The most

precious things of life are near at hand.
Each of you has the whole wealth
of the Universe at your very door.
All may be yours by stretching forth
your hand and taking it.

JOHN BURROUGHS

This is good

An old story is told of a king in Africa who had a close friend with whom he grew up. The friend had a habit of looking at every situation that ever occurred in his life (positive or negative) and remarking, "This is good!"

One day the king and his friend were out on a hunting expedition. The friend would load and prepare the guns for the king. The friend had apparently done something wrong in preparing one of the guns, for after taking the gun from his friend, the king fired it and his thumb was blown off.

Examining the situation the friend remarked as usual, "This is good!" To which the king replied, "No, this is NOT good!" and proceeded to send his friend to jail.
About a year later, the king was hunting in an area that he should have known to stay clear of. Cannibals captured him and took him to their village. They tied his hands, stacked some wood, set up a stake and bound him to the stake. As they came near to set fire to the wood, they noticed that the king was missing a thumb. Being superstitious, they never ate anyone that was less than whole. So untying the king, they sent him on his way.

As he returned home, he was reminded of the event that had taken his thumb and felt remorse for his treatment of his friend. He went immediately to the jail to speak with his friend. "You were right," he said, "it was good that my thumb was blown off."

And he proceeded to tell the friend all that had just happened. "And so I am very sorry for sending you to jail for so long. It was bad for me to do this." "No," his friend replied, "This is good!" "What do you mean, 'This is good'? How could it be good that I sent my friend to jail for a year?"

"If I had NOT been in jail, I would have been with you.

I told GOD...Let all my friends be healthy and happy forever...!
GOD said: But for 4 days only....!

I said: Yes, let them be a Spring Day, Summer Day, Autumn Day, and Winter Day.
GOD said: 3 days..

I said: Yes, Yesterday, Today and Tomorrow.
GOD said: No, 2 days!

I said: Yes, a Bright Day (Daytime) and Dark Day (Night-time).
GOD said: No, just 1 day!

I said: Yes!
GOD asked: Which day?

I said: Every Day in the living years of all my friends!
GOD laughed, and said:
All your friends will be healthy and happy Every Day.

A good lesson

A young man, a student in one of our universities, was one day taking a walk with a professor, who was commonly called the students' friend, from his kindness to those who waited on his instructions. As they went along, they saw lying in the path a pair of old shoes, which they supposed to belong to a poor man who was employed in a field close by, and who had nearly finished his day's work.

The student turned to the professor, saying: "Let us play the man a trick: we will hide his shoes, and conceal ourselves behind those bushes, and wait to see his perplexity when he cannot find them."

"My young friend," answered the professor, "we should never amuse ourselves at the expense of the poor. But you are rich, and may give yourself a much greater pleasure by means of the poor man. Put a coin into each shoe, and then we will hide ourselves and watch how the discovery affects him."

The student did so, and they both placed themselves behind the bushes close by. The poor man soon finished his work, and came across the field to the path where he had left his coat and shoes. While putting on his coat he slipped his foot into one of his shoes; but feeling something hard, he stooped down to feel what it was, and found the coin. Astonishment and wonder were seen upon his countenance. He gazed upon the coin, turned it round, and looked at it again and again. He then looked around him on all sides, but no person was to be seen. He now put the money into his pocket, and proceeded to put on the other shoe; but his surprise was doubled on finding the other coin. His feelings overcame him; he fell upon his knees, looked up to heaven and uttered aloud a fervent thanksgiving, in which he spoke of his wife, sick and helpless, and his children without bread, whom the timely bounty, from some unknown hand, would save from perishing.

The student stood there deeply affected, and his eyes filled with tears. "Now," said the professor, "are you not much better pleased than if you had played your intended trick?"

The youth replied, "You have taught me a lesson which I will never forget. I feel now the truth of those words, which I never understood before: 'It is more blessed to give than to receive.'"

Testament of Faith

You see I have some reason to wish that, in a future state, I may not only be as well as I was, but a little better. And I hope for it; for I...trust in God. And when I observe that there is great frugality, as well as wisdom in His works, since He has been evidently sparing both of labor and materials; for by the various wonderful inventions of propagation He has provided for the continual peopling of His world with plants and animals, without being at the trouble of repeated new creations; and by the natural reduction of compound substances to their original elements, capable of being employed in new compositions, he has prevented necessity of creating new matter; so that the earth, water air and perhaps fire, which being compounded from wood, do, when the wood is dissolved and again become air, earth, fire and water; I say that when I see nothing annihilated, and not ever a drop of water wasted, I cannot suspect the annihilation of souls; or believe that He will suffer the daily waste of millions of minds ready made that now exist and put Himself to the continual trouble of making new ones. Thus finding myself to exist in the world, I believe I shall in some shape or other, always exist; and, with all the inconveniences human life is liable to, I shall not object to a new edition of mine; hoping, however, that the errata of the last may be corrected.

BENJAMIN FRANKLIN'S LETTER TO GEORGE WHATLEY, 1785

Be like the sun for grace and mercy.
Be like the night to cover others' faults.
Be like running water for generosity.
Be like death for rage and anger.
Be like the Earth for modesty.
Appear as you are.
Be as you appear."

MAULANA JALAL-AL-DIN RUMI

Pictures of happiness

Sunbeams dancing
Horses prancing
Dragonfly flitting
Buddha sitting
Cats purring
Wheels whirring
Birds singing
Bells ringing
Snowball fighting
Candle lighting
Flower smelling
Story telling
Baby cuddles
Jumping in puddles
Singing in the rain
Strolling down memory lane

PAULINE OLIVER

Just a thought

O the miles that stretch between us
Just seem longer every day;
May you find a joy in knowing
That you're just a thought away.
Many miles may separate us
And the clouds between be grey
But you're cherished in my heart, dear,
And you're just a thought away.

GLENNA HULL

Conscience is what hurts when everything else feels so good.

Talk is cheap because supply exceeds demand.

Even if you are on the right track, you'll get run over if you just sit there.

An optimist thinks that this is the best possible world. A pessimist fears that this is true.

There is always death and taxes however death doesn't get worse every year.

People will accept your ideas much more readily if you tell them that Benjamin Franklin said it first.

You're getting old when you get the same sensation from a rocking chair that you once got from a roller coaster.

One of life's mysteries is how a two pound box of candy can make you gain five pounds.

A WOMAN'S ANSWER TO A MAN'S QUESTION

Do you know you have asked for the costliest thing
Ever made by the Hand above--
A woman's heart, and a woman's life,
And a woman's wonderful love?

Do you know you have asked for this priceless thing
As a child might ask for a toy?
Demanding what others have died to win,
With the reckless dash of a boy.

You have written my lesson of duty out,
Man-like you have questioned me;
Now stand at the bar of my woman's soul,
Until I shall question thee.

You require your mutton shall always be hot,
Your socks and your shirts shall be whole;
I require your heart shall be true as God's stars;
And pure as heaven your soul.

You require a cook for your mutton and beef;
I require far grander a thing;
A seamstress you're wanting for stockings and shirts--
I look for a man and a king.

A king for a beautiful realm called home,
And a man that the maker, God,
Shall look upon as he did the first,
And say, "It is very good."

I am fair and young, but the rose will fade
From my soft, young cheek one day;
Will you love me then, 'mid the falling leaves,
As you did 'mid the bloom of May?

Is your heart an ocean so strong and deep
I may launch my all on its tide?
A loving woman finds heaven or hell
On the day she is made a bride.

I require all things that are grand and true,
All things that a man should be;
If you give this all I would stake my life
To be all you demand of me.

If you cannot do this, a laundress and cook
You can hire with little to pay;
But a woman's heart and a woman's life
Are not to be won that way.

MARY T LATHRAP

FAILURE isn't fatal

Too often, it seems to me, people lose their courage in facing life because of past failures of fear that they may fail in the future. One good way to cure such fears is to remember the story of a man who actually built a lifetime of accomplishments out of defeats. The following litany of failures that punctuated his life throughout thirty years is a living and eloquent example of the successful use of defeat in achieving victory. Abraham Lincoln's record is as follows:

1. Lost job, 1832
2. Defeat for legislature, 1832
3. Failed in business, 1833
4. Elected to legislature, 1834
5. Sweetheart died, 1835
6. Had nervous breakdown. 1836
7. Defeated for speaker, 1838
8. Defeated for congress nomination, 1843
9. Elected to congress, 1846
10. Lost renomination, 1848
11. Rejected for land officer, 1849

12. Defeated for Senate, 1854
13. Defeated for nomination for Vice-President, 1856
14. Again defeated for Senate, 1858
15. Elected President of United States, 1860

Lincoln's deep conviction that God had given him a mission to fulfill accounted in no small way for his deep humility and ability to push on in the face of difficulties and failures that would have discouraged most people. His abiding faith was well summed up in this comment which he made after becoming President: "God selects his own instruments, and sometimes they are queer ones; for instance, He chose me to steer the ship through a great crisis."

You, too, in God's providence, can be instrument in bringing His love, truth and peace to a world in urgent need of it. And with Abraham Lincoln, you too can learn to say:

"With God's help I shall not fail"

REVEREND JAMES KELLER, M.M.

Friendship

Oh, the comfort
the inexpressible comfort
of feeling safe with a person,
Having neither to weigh
thoughts,
Nor measure words
but pouring them
All right out
just as they are
Chaff and grain together
Certain that a faithful hand will
Take and sift them
Keep what is worth keeping
And with the breath of
kindness
Blow the rest away.

DINAH MARIA MULOCK CRAIK

When you get to your wit's end,
you'll find God lives there.

We are living in world of beauty but how few of us open our eyes to eyes see it! What a different place this would be if our senses were trained to see and hear! We are the heirs of wonderful treasures from the past: treasures of literature and of the arts. They are ours fro the asking—all our own to have to enjoy, if only we desire them enough.

LORADO TAFT

Meet The Old Man

The father of Success is named Work; the mother is named Ambition. The oldest son is Common Sense and the other brothers are called Perseverance, Honesty, Thoughtfulness, Foresight, Enthusiasm, and Co-operation. Some of the sisters are Cheerfulness, Loyalty, Care, Courtesy, Economy, Sincerity and the "Old Man" and you will be able to get along with the rest of the family.

The real art of conversation is
not only to say the right thing
at the right time,
but also to leave unsaid
the wrong thing
at the tempting moment.

You don't stop laughing
because you grow old,
you grow old
because you stopped laughing.

I started out with nothing
and still have most of it left.

Quit griping about your church
if it was perfect, you couldn't belong.

Just For Today

Just for today I will try to live through this day only, and not tackle my whole life problem at once. I can do something for twelve hours that would appall me if I felt that I had to keep it up for a lifetime.

Just for today I will be happy. This assumes to be true what Abraham Lincoln said "most folks are as happy as they make up their minds to be." Just for today I will adjust myself to what is, and not try to adjust everything to my own desires. I will take my "luck" as it comes, and fit myself to it.

Just for today I will try to strengthen my mind. I will study. I will learn something useful. I will not be a mental loafer. I will read something that requires effort, thought and concentration.

Just for today, I will exercise my soul in three ways. I will do somebody a good turn, and not get found out; if anybody knows of it, it will not count. I will do at least two things I don't want to do – just for exercise. I will not show anyone that my feelings are hurt; they may be hurt, but today I will not show it.

Just for today I will be agreeable. I will look as well as I can, dress becomingly, talk low, act courteously, criticize not one bit, not find fault with anything, nor try to improve or regulate anybody except myself.

Just for today I will have a program. I may not follow it exactly, but I will have it. I will save myself from two pests – hurry and indecision.

Just for today I will a quiet half-hour all by myself and relax. During this half-hour, some time, I will try to get a better perspective of my life.

Just for today I will doo unto you, as I would have done unto me. I will think of you, as I would have you think of me and I will speak of you, as I would have you speak of me. But before I speak of you, I will ask myself these questions: "Is it good?" "Is it necessary?"

Just for today I will be unafraid. Especially I will not be afraid to enjoy that which is beautiful, and to believe that as I give to the world, so the world will give to me.

Every moment is a golden one
for him who has the vision to
recognize it as such.
HENRY MILLER

If we are strong from within,
there is nothing from without
that can harm us.

The minute you settle for less
than you deserve, you get
even less than you settled for.
**MAUREEN DOWD, IN 'NEW YORK
TIMES'**

Until you become prosperous,
you'll never know how many
"old friends" you have.

The thing I hate about an
argument is that it always
interrupts a discussion.
G. K. CHESTERTON

A lot of little prayers as we go
along would save a great long
one in case of emergency.

That's what I consider true
generosity. You give your all,
and yet you always feel as if it
costs you nothing.
SIMONE DE BEAUVOIR

Man spends his life reasoning
on the past, complaining of
the present, and trembling for
the future.

The Splashes of Life

To each man's life
there comes a time supreme,
One day, one night, one morning,
or one noon,
One freighted hour,
one moment opportune,
One space when faith
goes tiding with the stream.
Happy the man who,
knowing how to wait,
Knows also how to watch,
and work, and stand
On life's broad deck alert,
and on the prow
To seize the passing moment
big with fate
From opportunity's extended hand
When the great clock of destiny strikes

Now.

A friend is someone we turn to
when our spirits need a lift.
A friend is someone we treasure
for our friendship is a gift.
A friend is someone
who fills our lives
with beauty, joy, and grace.
And makes
the whole world we live in
a better and happier place.
JEAN KYLER MCMANUS

*Forgiveness
is a funny thing.
It warms the heart
and cools the sting.*

WILLIAM ARTHUR WARD

Watch the corners

When you wake up in the morning of a chill and cheerless day,
And feel inclined to grumble, pout or frown,
Just glance into your mirror and you will quickly see
It's just because the corners of your mouth turn down.
If you wake up in the morning full of bright and happy thoughts,
And begin to count the blessing in your cup,
Then glance into your mirror and you will quickly see
Its all because the corners of your mouth turn up.
Then take this little rhyme,
Remember all the time:
There's joy a-plenty in this world to fill life's silver cup
If you'll only keep the corners of your mouth turned up.

LULU LINTON

Growing Good Corn

James Bender, in his book How to Talk Well (published in 1994 by McGraw-Hill Book Company Inc.) relates the story of a farmer who grew award-winning corn. Each year he entered his corn in the state fair where it won a blue ribbon.

One year a newspaper reporter interviewed him and learned something interesting about how he grew it. The reporter discovered that the farmer shared his seed corn with his neighbours.

'How can you afford to share your best seed corn with your neighbours when they are entering corn in competition with yours each year?' the reporter asked.

'Why sir,' said the farmer, 'didn't you know? The wind picks up pollen from the ripening corn and swirls it from field to field. If my neighbours grow inferior corn, cross-pollination will steadily degrade the quality of my corn. If I am to grow good corn, I must help my neighbours grow good corn.'

He is very much aware of the connectedness of life. His corn cannot improve unless his neighbour's corn also improves.

So it is in other dimensions of our lives.

Those who choose to be at peace, must help their neighbours to be at peace.

Those who choose to live well must help others to live well, for the value of a life is measured by the lives it touches.

And those who choose to be happy must help others to find happiness, for the welfare of each is bound up with the welfare of all.

The lesson for each of us is this . . . if we are to grow good corn, we must help our neighbours grow good corn.

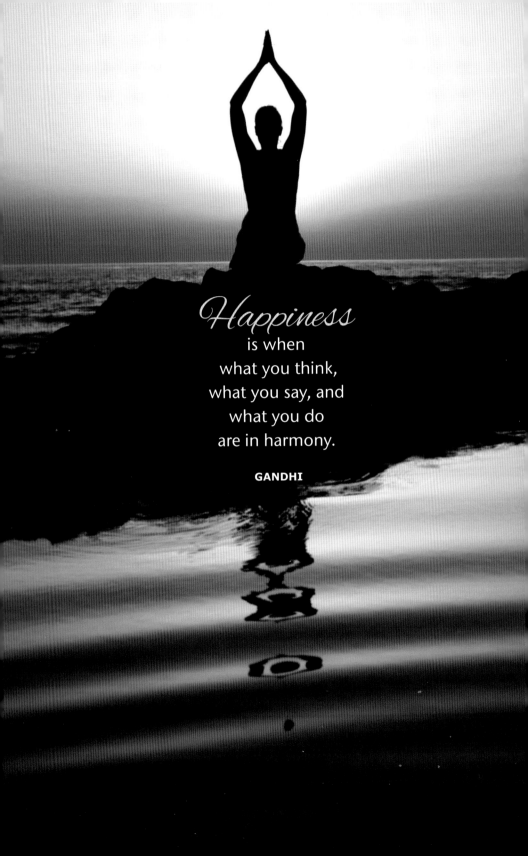

Happiness
is when
what you think,
what you say, and
what you do
are in harmony.

GANDHI

The Loom of Time

Man's life is laid in the loom of time
To a pattern he does not see,
While the weavers work and the shuttles fly
Till the dawn of eternity.
Some shuttles are filled with silver threads
And some with threads of gold,
While often but the darker hues
Are all that they may hold.
But the weaver watches with skillful eye
Each shuttle fly to and fro,
And sees the pattern so deftly wrought
As the loom moves sure and slow.
God surely planned the pattern:
Each thread, the dark and fair,
Is chosen by His master skill
And placed in the web with care.
He only knows its beauty,
And guides the shuttles which hold
The threads so unattractive,
As well as the threads of gold.
Not till each loom is silent,
And the shuttles cease to fly,
Shall God reveal the pattern
And explain the reason why
The dark threads were as needful
In the weaver's skillful hand
As the threads of gold and silver
For the pattern which He planned.

Don't Quit

*A*s a kid, growing up in a home filled with books, I was always drawn to the written word. At the age of 12, I was in a used paper and bookstore near my house. Going through the shelves, I found an old diary in which I read this poem that set me on a path of enjoying inspirational poems and enriching my life. The diary had been discarded, but to me this poem is still refreshing. The diary belonged to my neighbor, Philomena Serrao. Over the years, I have read many a poem that has inspired me, but this one still happens to be my favorite. Thank you Philoo for writing that poem down in your diary.

Don't Quit

When things go wrong, as they sometimes will,
When the road you're trudging seems all uphill,
When the funds are low and the debts are high,
And you want to smile, but you have to sigh,
When care is pressing you down a bit,
Rest, if you must, but do not quit.
Life is queer with its twists and turns,
As every one of us sometimes learns,
And many a failure turns about,
When he might have won had he stuck it out,
Don't give up though the pace seems slow—
You may succeed with another blow.
Often the goal is nearer than,
It seems to a faint and faltering man,
Often the struggler has given up,
When he might have captured the victor's cup,
And he learned too late when the night slipped down,
How close he was to the golden crown.
Success is failure turned inside out—
The silver tint of the clouds of doubt,
And you never can tell how close you are,
It may be near when it seems so far,
So stick to the fight when you're hardest hit—
It's when things seem worst that you must not quit.

The Obstacle in Our Path

In ancient times, a king had a boulder placed on a roadway. Then he hid himself and watched to see if anyone would remove the huge rock.

Some of the king's wealthiest merchants and courtiers came by and simply walked around it. Many loudly blamed the king for not keeping the roads clear, but none did anything about getting the big stone out of the way.

Then a peasant came along carrying a load of vegetables. On approaching the boulder, the peasant laid down his burden and tried to move the stone to the side of the road. After much pushing and straining, he finally succeeded.

As the peasant picked up his load of vegetables, he noticed a purse lying in the road where the boulder had been. The purse contained many gold coins and a note from the king indicating that the gold was for the person who removed the boulder from the roadway.

The peasant learned what many others never understand.

Every obstacle presents an opportunity to improve one's condition.

A very old story.

It is easier to get older than it is to get wiser.

Give God what's right not what's left.

Man's way leads to a hopeless end God's way leads to an endless hope.

A lot of kneeling will keep you in good standing.

He who kneels before God can stand before anyone.

In the sentence of life, the devil may be a comma but never let him be the period.

When praying, don't give God instructions just report for duty.

Plan ahead It wasn't raining when Noah built the ark.

Most people want to serve God, but only in an advisory position.

The Picture Of The Praying Hands

They tossed a coin on a Sunday morning after church. Albrecht Durer won the toss and went off to Nuremberg. Albert went down into the dangerous mines and, for the next four years, financed his brother, whose work at the academy was almost an immediate sensation. Albrecht's etchings, his woodcuts, and his oils were far better than those of most of his professors, and by the time he graduated, he was beginning to earn considerable fees for his commissioned works.

When the young artist returned to his village, the Durer family held a festive dinner on their lawn to celebrate Albrecht's triumphant homecoming. After a long and memorable meal, punctuated with music and laughter, Albrecht rose from his honored position at the head of the table to drink a toast to his beloved brother for the years of sacrifice that had enabled Albrecht to fulfill his ambition.

His closing words were, "And now, Albert, blessed brother of mine, now it is your turn. Now you can go to Nuremberg to pursue your dream, and I will take care of you." All heads turned in eager expectation to the far end of the table where Albert sat, tears streaming down his pale face, shaking his lowered head from side to side while he sobbed and repeated, over and over, "No ...no ...no ...no."

Finally, Albert rose and wiped the tears from his cheeks. He glanced down the long table at the faces he loved, and then, holding his hands close to his right cheek, he said softly, "No, brother.. I cannot go to Nuremberg. It is too late for me. Look ... look what four years in the mines have done to my hands! The bones in every finger have been smashed at least once, and lately I have been suffering from arthritis so badly in my right hand that I cannot even hold a glass to return your toast, much less make delicate lines on parchment or canvas with a pen or a brush. No, brother ... for me it is too late."

More than 475 years have passed. By now, Albrecht Durers hundreds of masterful portraits, pen and silver-point sketches, watercolors, charcoals, woodcuts, and copper engravings hang in every great museum in the world, but the odds are great that you, like most people, are familiar with only one of Albrecht Durers works. More than merely being familiar with it, you very well may have a reproduction hanging in your home or office.

One day, to pay homage to Albert for all that he had sacrificed, Albrecht Durer painstakingly drew his brothers abused hands with palms together and thin fingers stretched skyward. He called his powerful drawing simply "Hands," but the entire world almost immediately opened their hearts to his great masterpiece and renamed his tribute of love, "The Praying Hands."

The next time you see a copy of that touching creation, take a second look Let it be your reminder, if you still need one, that no one - no one - ever makes it alone!

The Bible is full of promises for those who seek it. I have enjoyed the strength of the twenty third psalm thanks to my mother. Here are some of those promises :

"It's impossible" - All things are possible
(LUKE 18:27)

"I'm too tired" - I will give you rest
(MATTHEW 11:28-30)

"Nobody really loves me" - I love you
(JOHN 3:16)

"I can't go on" - My grace is sufficient
(II COR. 12:19)

"I can't figure things out" - I will guide your steps
(PROVERBS 20:24)

"I can't do it" - You can do all things
(PHIL 4:13)

"I'm not able" - I am able
(II COR. 9:8)

"It's not worth it" - It will be worth it
(ROMANS 8:28)

"I can't forgive myself" - I forgive you
(I JOHN 1:9 & ROMANS 8:1)

"I can't manage" - I will supply all your needs
(PHIL. 4:19)

"I'm afraid" - I have not given you a spirit of fear
(II TIM. 1:7)

"I'm always worried and frustrated" - Cast all your cares on Me
(I PETER 5:7)

"I don't have enough faith" - I've given everyone a measure of faith
(ROMANS 12:8)

"I'm not smart enough" - I give you wisdom
(I COR. 1:30)

"I feel all alone" - I will never leave you or forsake you
(HEBREWS 13:5)

Take time to live;
The world has much to give,
Of faith and hope and love;
Of faith that life is good,
That human brotherhood
Shall no illusion prove;
Of hope that future years
Shall bring the best, in spite
Of those whose darkened sight
Would stir our doubts and fears;
Of love, that makes of life,
With all its grief's, a song;
A friend, of conquered wrong;
A symphony, of strife.
Take time to live,
Nor to vain mammon five
Your fruitful years.

Take time to live;
The world has much to give
Of sweet content; of joy
At duty bravely done;
Of hope, that every sun
Shall bring more fair employ.
Take time to live,
For life has much to give
Despite the cynic's sneer
That all's forever wrong;
There's much that calls for song.
To fate lend not your ear.
The world has much to give.

THOMAS CURTIS CLARK

*Never mess up an apology
with an excuse.*

Lately, I am reading a lot on Gandhi the saint of India. While visiting my brother Chetan, I was lucky to find a bookstore solely dedicated to Gandhi in Bombay. Here is one lovely incident in the life of this truly great soul.

As Gandhi stepped aboard a train one day, one of his shoes slipped off and landed on the track. He was unable to retrieve it as the train started rolling. To the amazement of his companions, Gandhi calmly took off his other shoe and threw it back along the track to land close to the first shoe.

Asked by a fellow passenger why he did that, Gandhi replied, "The poor man who finds the shoe lying on the track will now have a pair he can use."

Where there is Faith, There is Love.
Where there is Love, There is Peace.
Where there is Peace, There is God.
Where there is God, There is no need.

For what is faith
unless it is to believe what you do not see?

SAINT AUGUSTINE

Ten rules for *Happier Living*

1. Give something away (no strings attached).

2. Do a kindness (and forget it).

3. Spend a few minutes with the aged (their experience is a priceless guidance).

4. Look intently into the face of a baby (and marvel).

5. Laugh often (it's life's lubricant).

6. Give thanks (a thousand times a day is not enough).

7. Pray (or you will lose the way).

8. Work (with whim and vigor).

9. Plan as though you'll live forever (because your memory and work will).

10. Live humbly as though you'll die tomorrow (because you will on some tomorrow).

A sincere heart prays

Founded by the romans around 70 A.D, this little village in England is now a busy city, and a popular European destinaton, where Daniel Craig, the present James Bond, was born.

Having been a well established place over centuries, there are many churches and cathedrals that are a part of its history. Chiseled on the wall of one of these cathedrals is this wonderful prayer:

"The Ideal State"

Give me a good digestion Lord,
and something to digest;
Give me a healthy body Lord,
and sense to keep it at its best;

Give me a healthy mind, O Lord,
to keep the good and pure in sight,
which seeing sin, is not appalled,
but finds a way to set it right.

Give me a mind that is not bored,
that does not whimper, whine or sigh;
Don't let me worry overmuch
about that fussy thing called "I";

Give me a sense of humor, Lord -
give me the grace to see a joke,
To get some happiness in life
and pass it on to other folk.

85

God's bank ain't busted yet!

Millions of americans are suffering from job loss, downsizing at work, lesser work hours, and financial strain. These are indeed hard times, but we must not give in to the negative strain in this otherwise glorious life. Giving up is the easiest thing to do, but it is not the solution. We must work harder at work, be more punctual, and let our efficiency show that we are needed. If necessary, we should be willing to put in extra effort, so that our work "makes a difference" in the big scheme of things. Alice P. Mossin, wrote this wonderfully inspiring poem seventy five years ago during the hard years of depression whose words are so needed even today .

The bank had closed; my earthly store had vanished from my hand;
I felt that there was no sadder one than I in all the land.
My washerwoman, too, had lost her little mite with mine,
And she was singing as she hung the clothes upon the line.
"How can you be so happy?" I asked;
"Your loss don't you regret?"
"Yes, Ma'm, but what's the use to fret?
God's bank ain't busted yet!"

I felt my burden lighter grow; her faith I seemed to share;
In prayer I went to God's great throne and laid my troubles there.
The sun burst from behind the clouds, in golden splendour set;
I thanked God for her simple words:
"God's bank ain't busted yet!"

And now I draw rich dividends, more than my hands can hold
Of faith and love and hope and trust and peace of mind untold.
I thank the Giver of it all, but still I can't forget
My washerwoman's simple words:
"God's bank ain't busted yet!"

Oh, weary ones upon life's road, when everything seems drear,
And losses loom on every hand, and skies seem not to clear;
Throw back your shoulder, lift your head, and cease to chafe and fret
Your dividend will bedeclared:
"God's bank ain't busted yet!"

"This country was not built by men who relied on somebody else to take care of them. It was built by men who relied on themselves, who dared to shape their own lives, who had enough courage to blaze new trails-enough confidence in themselves to take necessary risks."

J. OLLIE EDMUNDS

I'm sharing this quote because to me, it exemplifies what is missing and what most have forgotten. As Americans we want what is easy and we have become followers and have become accepting of things that are wrong and have tolerated it. We are relying to much on others.

True leaders are hard to find and you know that, people unafraid, and that needs to change. Not just in actions, but in our thinking. To get back to what made America the way it is today. Finding this, I believe we develop people with character and confidence, and in turn, leaders.

CURT

Made Where?

Larry Smith started the day early having set his alarm clock (MADE IN JAPAN) for 6 a.m. While his coffee pot (MADE IN CHINA) was perking, he shaved with his electric razor (MADE IN HONG KONG). He put on a dress shirt (MADE IN SRI LANKA), designer jeans (MADE IN SINGAPORE) and tennis shoes (MADE IN KOREA).

After cooking his breakfast in his new electric skillet (MADE IN CHINA) he sat down with his calculator (MADE IN MEXICO) to see how much he could spend today. After setting his watch (MADE IN TAIWAN) to the radio (MADE IN MEXICO) he got in his car (MADE IN GERMANY), turned on his mp3 player (MADE IN CHINA) and continued his search for a good paying AMERICAN JOB. At the end of yet another discouraging and fruitless day, Joe decided to relax for a while. He put on his sandals (MADE IN BRAZIL), a soft cotton shirt (MADE IN PHILLIPINES), he poured himself a glass of wine (MADE IN FRANCE) and turned on his TV (MADE IN CHINA), and listened to an infomercial about a new gadget hosted by an european sounding guy and then wondered why he can't find a good paying job in.....AMERICA.....

THIS means unless we start producing and manufacturing for less, we will even import our butter from overseas. Something to think about.

Preserve sacredly the privacies of your own house,
your married state and your heart.
Let no father or mother or sister or brother
ever presume to come between you
or share the joys or sorrows
that belong to you two alone.

With mutual help to build your quiet world,
not allowing your dearest earthly friend
to be the confidant of aught
that concerns your domestic peace.

Let moments of alienation,
if they occur, be healed at once.
Never, no never, speak of it outside;
but to each other confess
and all will come out all right.

Never let the morrow's sun
still find you at variance.
Renew and renew your vow.
It will do you good,
and thereby
your minds will grow together
contented in that love
which is stronger than death,
and you will be truly one.

Psalm 23

My mother, who introduced this wonderful psalm to me a few years back, explained to me the promises and the assurances given by God to us in these words of David. Thank you, dear mumma. I am sharing them with my readers.

The Lord is my Shepherd

That's Relationship!

I shall not want

That's Supply!

He maketh me to lie down
in green pastures.

That's Rest!

He leadeth me beside
the still waters.

That's Refreshment!

He restoreth my soul

That's Healing!

He leadeth me in the paths
of righteousness.

That's Guidance!

For His name sake

That's Purpose!

Yea, though I walk through the valley
of the shadow of death.

That's Testing!

I will fear no evil.

That's Protection!

For Thou art with me

That's Faithfulness!

Thy rod and Thy staff
they comfort me,

That's Discipline!

Thou preparest a table before me
in the presence of my enemies.

That's Hope!

Thou anointest my head with oil,

That's Consecration!

My cup runneth over.

That's Abundance!

Surely goodness and mercy
shall follow me all the days of my life.

That's Blessing!

And I will dwell in the house
of the Lord.

That's Security!

Forever.

That's Eternity!

Dear God

I'm writing to say I'm sorry
for being angry yesterday
when you seemed to ignore
my prayer and things didn't
go my way

My car broke down
I was very late for work
but I missed that awful accident
was that your handiwork?

I know you're watching over me
and I'm feeling truly blessed
for no matter what I pray for
you always know what's best!

Imagination

is what makes the average men
think he can run the business so
much better than his boss.

Be not anxious about tomorrow.
Do today's duty, fight today's
temptation, and do not weaken
and distract yourself by looking
forward to things which you can-
not see, and could not understand
if you saw them.

CHARLES KINGSLEY

To love life

to love it even
when you have no stomach for it
and everything you've held dear
crumbles like burnt paper in your hands,
your throat filled with the silt of it.
When grief sits with you, its tropical heat
thickening the air, heavy as water
more fit for gills than lungs;
when grief weights you like your own flesh
only more of it, an obesity of grief,
you think, How can a body withstand this?
Then you hold life like a face
between your palms, a plain face,
no charming smile, no violet eyes,
and you say, yes, I will take you
I will love you, again.

ELLEN BASS

"My Lord God, I have no idea where I am going, I do not see the road ahead of me, I cannot know for certain where it will end. Nor do I really know myself, and the fact that I think I am following your will does not mean that I am actually doing so. But I believe that the desire to please you does in fact please you. And I hope I have that desire in all that I am doing. I hope that I will never do anything apart from that desire. And I know that if I do this you will lead me by the right road, though I may know nothing about it. Therefore, I will trust you always, though I may seem to be lost and in the shadow of death. I will not fear, for you are ever with me, and you will never leave me to face my perils alone."

THOMAS MERTON

If I have learned anything

I've learned that heroes are the people who do what has to be done, when it needs to be done, regardless of the consequences.

I've learned that when the light turns green,
you had better look both ways before proceeding.

I've learned that you can love someone
and still not like them very much.

I've learned that there are people who love you dearly,
but just don't know how to show it.

I've learned that my best friend and I
can do anything or nothing and still have the best time.

I've learned that sometimes the people you expect
to kick you when you're down will be the ones to help you get back up.

I've learned that I'm getting more and more like my mom,
and I'm kind of happy about it.

I've learned that sometimes when I'm angry, I have the right to be angry,
but that doesn't give me the right to be cruel.

I've learned that true friendship continues to grow,
even over the longest distance.

I've learned that just because someone doesn't love you the way you
want them to doesn't mean they don't love you with all they have.

I've learned that no matter how much I care,
some people just don't care back.

Children learn...
what they live with

If a child lives with criticism,
He learns to condemn.
If a child lives with hostility,
He learns to fight.
If a child live with fear,
He learns to be apprehensive.
If a child lives with pity,
He learns to feel sorry for himself.
If a child lives with jealousy,
He learns to envy.
If a child lives with encouragement
He learns to be confident.
If a child lives with tolerance,
He learns to be patient.
If a child lives with praise,
He learns to be appreciative.
If a child lives with acceptance.
He learns to love.
If a child lives with approval,
He learns to like himself.
If a child lives with recognition,
He learns to have a goal.
If a child lives with fairness,
He learns what justice is.
If a child lives with honesty,
He learns what the truth is.
If a child lives with security,
He learns to have faith in himself
and those about him.
If a child lives with friendliness,
He learns the world is
a nice place in which to live.
If you are the parent,
With what is your child living?

Turning Things Around

1. Pray
2. Go to bed on time.
3. Get up on time so you can start the day unrushed.
4. Say No to projects that won't fit into your time schedule, or that will compromise your mental health.
5. Delegate tasks to capable others.
6. Simplify and un-clutter your life.
7. Less is more. (Although one is often not enough, two are often too many).
8. Allow extra time to do things and to get to places.
9. Pace yourself. Spread out big changes and difficult projects over time; don't lump the hard things all together.
10. Take one day at a time.
11. Separate worries from concerns. If a situation is a concern, find out what God would have you do and let go of the anxiety. If you can't do anything about a situation, forget it.
12. Live within your budget; don't use credit cards for ordinary purchases.
13. Have backups; an extra car key in your wallet, an extra house key buried in the garden, extra stamps, etc.
14. K.M.S. (Keep Mouth Shut). This single piece of advice can prevent an enormous amount of trouble.
15. Do something for the Kid in You everyday.
16. Carry an inspirational book with you to read while waiting in line.
17. Get enough rest.

18. Eat right.
19. Get organized so everything has its place.
20. Listen to something while driving that can help improve your quality of life.
21. Write down thoughts and inspirations.
22. Every day, find time to be alone.
23. Having problems? Talk to God on the spot. Try to nip small problems in the bud. Don't wait until it's time to go to bed to try and pray.
24. Make friends with Godly people.
25. Keep a folder of favorite scriptures on hand.
26. Remember that the shortest bridge between despair and hope is often a good 'Thank you God.'
27. Laugh.
28. Laugh some more!
29. Take your work seriously, but not yourself at all.
30. Develop a forgiving attitude (most people are doing the best they can).
31. Be kind to unkind people (they probably need it the most).
32. Sit on your ego.
33. Talk less; listen more.
34. Slow down.
35. Remind yourself that you are not the general manager of the universe.
36. Every night before bed, think of one thing you're grateful for that you've never been grateful for before.

The Tone of Voice

It's not so much what your say
As the manner in which you say it;
It's not so much the language you use
As the tone in which you convey it;
"Come here!" I sharply said,
And the child cowered and wept.
"Come here," I said -
He looked and smiled
And straight to my lap he crept.
Words may be mild and fair
And the tone may pierce like a dart;
Words may be soft as the summer air
But the tome may break my heart;
For words come from the mind
Grow by study and art -
But tone leaps from the inner self
Revealing the state of the heart.
Whether you know it or not,
Whether you mean or care,
Gentleness, kindness, love, and hate,
Envy, anger, are there.
Then, would you quarrels avoid
And peace and love rejoice?
Keep anger nor only out of your words -
Keep it out of your voice.

A man was exploring caves by the seashore. In one of the caves he found a canvas bag with a bunch of hardened clay balls. It was like someone had rolled clay balls and left them out in the sun to bake.

They didn't look like much, but they intrigued the man, so he took the bag out of the cave with him. As he strolled along the beach, he would throw the clay balls one at a time out into the ocean as far as he could.

He thought little about it, until he dropped one of the clay balls and it cracked open on a rock. Inside was a beautiful, precious stone!

Excited, the man started breaking open the remaining clay balls. Each contained a similar treasure. He found thousands of dollars worth of jewels in the 20 or so clay balls he had left. Then it struck him.

He had been on the beach a long time. He had thrown maybe 50 or 60 of the clay balls with their hidden treasure into the ocean waves. Instead of thousands of dollars in treasure, he could have taken home tens of thousands, but he had just thrown it away!

It's like that with people. We look at someone, maybe even ourselves, and we see the external clay vessel. It doesn't look like much from the outside. It isn't always beautiful or sparkling, so we discount it. We see that person as less important than someone more beautiful or stylish or well known or wealthy. But we have not taken the time to find the treasure hidden inside that person.

There is a treasure in each and every one of us. If we take the time to get to know that person, and if we ask God to show us that person the way He sees them, then the clay begins to peel away and the brilliant gem begins to shine forth.

May we not come to the end of our lives and find out that we have thrown away a fortune in friendships because the gems were hidden in bits of clay. May we see the people in our world as God sees them.

Don't cry because its over,
smile because it happened.

A Sunday school teacher was discussing the Ten Commandments with her five and six year olds.

After explaining the commandment to "honor" thy Father and thy mother," she asked, "is there a commandment that teaches us how to treat our brothers and sisters?"

Without missing a beat one little boy (the oldest of a family) answered, "Thou shalt not kill."

Everyone is a house with four rooms, a physical, a mental, an emotional and a spiritual.
Most of us tend to live in one room most of the time, but unless we go into every room, every day, even if only to keep it aired, we are not a complete person.

HINDU PROVERB

There are as many nights as days, and the one is just as long as the other in the year's course.
Even a happy life cannot be without a measure of darkness, and the word 'happy' would lose its meaning if it were not balanced by sadness.

CARL JUNG

The summit of happiness is reached when a person is ready to be what he is.

ERASMUS

Maybe this world is another planet's hell.
ALDOUS HUXLEY

To live a pure unselfish life, one must count nothing as one's own in the midst of abundance.
BUDDHA

Our own life is the instrument with which we experiment with the truth.
THICH NHAT HANH

The talent for being happy is appreciating and liking what you have, instead of what you don't have.
WOODY ALLEN

It is not how much we have, but how much we enjoy, that makes happiness.
CHARLES SPURGEON

We need not only a purpose in life to give meaning to our existence but also something to give meaning to our suffering
ERIC HOFFER

Down Memory Lane

A little house with three bedrooms and one car on the street,
A mower that you had to push to make the grass look neat.
In the kitchen on the wall we only had one phone,
And no need for recording things, someone was always home.

We only had a living room where we would congregate,
Unless it was at mealtime in the kitchen where we ate.
We had no need for family rooms or extra rooms to dine,
When meeting as a family those two rooms would work out fine.

We only had one TV set, and channels maybe two,
But always there was one of them with something worth the view.
For snacks we had potato chips that tasted like a chip,
And if you wanted flavor there was Lipton's onion dip.

Store-bought snacks were rare because my mother liked to cook,
And nothing can compare to snacks in Betty Crockery's book.
The snacks were even healthy with the best ingredients,
No labels with a hundred things that make not a bit of sense.

Weekends were for family trips or staying home to play,
We all did things together -- even go to church to pray.
When we did our weekend trips depending on the weather,
No one stayed at home because we liked to be together.

Sometimes we would separate to do things on our own,
But we knew where the others were without our own cell phone.
Then there were the movies with your favorite movie star,
And nothing can compare to watching movies in your car.

Then there were the picnics at the peak of summer season,
Pack a lunch and find some trees and never need a reason.
Get a baseball game together with all the friends you know,
Have real action playing ball -- and no game video.

Remember when the doctor used to be the family friend,
And didn't need insurance or a lawyer to defend?
The way that he took care of you or what he had to do,
Because he took an oath and strived to do the best for you.

Remember going to the store and shopping casually,
And when you went to pay for it you used your own money?
Nothing that you had to swipe or punch in some amount,
Remember when the cashier person had to really count?

Remember when we breathed the air; it smelled so fresh and clean,
And chemicals were not used on the grass to keep it green.
The milkman used to go from door to door,
And it was just a few cents more than going to the store.

There was a time when mailed letters came right to your door,
Without a lot of junk mail ads sent out by every store.
The mailman knew each house by name and knew where it was sent;
There were not loads of mail addressed to "present occupant."

Remember when the words "I do" meant that you really did,
And not just temporarily "til someone blows their lid."
T'was no such thing as "no one's fault; we just made a mistake,"
There was a time when married life was built on give and take.

There was a time when just one glance was all that it would take,
And you would know the kind of car, the model and the make.
They didn't look like turtles trying to squeeze out every mile;
They were streamlined, white walls, fins, and really had some style.

One time the music that you played whenever you would jive,
Was from a vinyl, big-holed record called a forty-five.
The record player had a post to keep them all in line,
And then the records would drop down and play one at a time.

Oh sure, we had our problems then, just like we do today,
And always we were striving, trying for a better way.
And every year that passed us by brought new and greater things,
We now can even program phones with music or with rings.

Oh, the simple life we lived still seems like so much fun,
How can you explain a game, just kick the can and run?
And why would boys put baseball cards between bicycle spokes,
And for a nickel red machines had little bottled Cokes?

This life seemed so much easier and slower in some ways,
I love the new technology but I sure miss those days.
So, time moves on and so do we, and nothing stays the same,
But I sure love to reminisce and walk down memory lane.

*God gave us memories
that we might have roses
in december.*
J.M. BARRIE

Ain't that the truth

If you're too open minded, your brains will fall out.

Age is a high price for maturity.

Artificial intelligence is no match for natural stupidity.

If you must choose between two evils, pick the one you have never tried before.

My idea of housework is to sweep the room with a glance.

Not one shred of evidence supports the notion that life is serious.

It is easier to get forgiveness than permission.

For every action, there is an equal and opposite government programme.

If you look like your passport picture, you probably need the trip. Bills travel through the post at twice the speed of cheques.

A conscience is what hurts when all your other parts feel so good.

Eat well, stay fit, die anyway.

Men are from Earth. Women are from Earth. Deal with it.

No husband has ever been shot while doing the dishes.

A balanced diet is a biscuit in each hand.

Opportunities always look bigger going than coming.

Middle age is when broadness of mind and narrowness of the waist change places.

Junk is something you've kept for years and throw away three weeks before you need it.

There is always one more imbecile than you counted on.

Experience is a wonderful thing. It enables you to recognise a mistake when you make it again.

By the time you can make ends meet, they move the ends.

Thou shalt not weigh more than thy refrigerator.

Someone who thinks logically provides a nice contrast to the real world.

Blessed are they who can laugh at themselves for they shall never cease to be amused.

An optimist is the man who thinks he can build a $200,000 house for $200,000.

Molehills of debt build mountains of worry.

You won't find success rules that work unless you do.

Instead of conting our blessings at the dinner table, most of us are busy counting calories.

Yuwa

A.S.A.P.

Ever wonder about the acronym,
A.S.A.P.?

Generally we think of it in terms of
even more hurry and stress in our
lives. Maybe if we think of this in a
different manner, we will begin to find
a new way to deal with those rough
days along the way.

There's work to do, deadlines to meet,
You've got no time to spare.
But as you hurry and scurry,
A.S.A.P. - ALWAYS SAY A PRAYER.

In the midst of family chaos,
"Quality time" is rare.
Do your best, let God do the rest,
A.S.A.P. - ALWAYS SAY A PRAYER.

It may seem like your worries
Are more than you can bear.
Slow down and take a breather,
A.S.A.P. - ALWAYS SAY A PRAYER.

God knows how stressful life is,
He wants to ease our cares.
And He'll respond to all your needs,
A.S.A.P. - ALWAYS SAY A PRAYER.

The 7 Ups

1. Wake Up - Decide to have a good day. "Today is the day the Lord hath made; let us rejoice & be glad in it" Psalms 118:24

2. Dress Up - The best way to dress up is to put on a smile. A smile is an inexpensive way to improve your looks. "The Lord does not look at the things man looks at. Man looks at outward appearance but the Lord looks at the heart" I Sam 16:7

3. Shut Up - Say nice things & learn to listen. God gave us 2 ears and 1 mouth so He must have meant for us to do twice as much listening as talking. "He who guards his lips guards his soul" Proverbs 13:3 "Gossip betrays confidence avoid men who talk too much" Proverbs 20:19 "Listen to advice, accept instruction and in the end, you will be wise" Proverbs 19:20

4. Stand Up - For what you believe in. Stand for something or you will fall for anything. "Let us not be weary in doing good; for at the proper time, we will reap a harvest if we do not give up. Therefore, as we have opportunity, let us do good..." Galatians 6:9-10

5. Look Up - To the Lord. "I can do everything through Him who gives me strength" Phillipians 4:13

6. Reach Up - For something higher. As Jiminy Cricket sings "High Hopes" Always try to better yourself. Have FAITH. "Now faith is being sure of what we hope for and certain of what we do not see." Hebrews 11:1

7. Lift Up - Your Prayers. "Do not worry about anything; instead PRAY ABOUT EVERYTHING" Phillipians 4:6

The splashes of life..

My grandfather took me to the fish pond on the farm when I was about seven, and he told me to throw a stone into the water. He told me to watch the circles created by the stone. Then he asked me to think of myself as that stone person.

"You may create lots of splashes in your life but the waves that come from those splashes will disturb the peace of all your fellow creatures," he said. "Remember that you are responsible for what you put in your circle and that circle will also touch many other circles. You will need to live in a way that allows the good that comes from your circle to send the peace of that goodness to others. The splash that comes from anger or jealousy will send those feelings to other circles. You are responsible for both."

That was the first time I realized each person creates the inner peace or discord that flows out into the world. We cannot create world peace if we are riddled with inner conflict, hatred, doubt, or anger. We radiate the feelings and thoughts that we hold inside, whether we speak them or not. Whatever is splashing around inside of us is spilling out into the world, creating beauty or discord with all other circles of life.

So, this explains the saying: WHATEVER YOU FOCUS ON, EXPANDS...

Life's Harmonies

Let no man pray that he know not sorrow,
Let no soul ask to be free from pain,
For the gall of to-day is the sweet of to-morrow,
And the moment's loss is the lifetime's gain.

Through want of a thing does its worth redouble,
Through hunger's pangs does the feast content,
And only the heart that has harbored trouble,
Can fully rejoice when joy is sent.

Let no man shrink from the bitter tonics
Of grief, and yearning, and need, and strife,
For the rarest chords in the soul's harmonies,
Are found in the minor strains of life.

ELLA WHEELER WILCOX

One day a little girl was sitting and watching her mother do the dishes at the kitchen sink. She suddenly noticed that her mother has several strands of white hair sticking out in contrast on her brunette head. She looked at her mother and inquisitively asked, "Why are some of your hairs white, Mom?" Her mother replied, "Well, every time that you do something wrong and make me cry or unhappy, one of my hairs turns white." The little girl thought about this revelation for a while and then said, "Momma, how come ALL of grandma's hairs are white?"

"A hero is no braver than an ordinary man,
but he is brave five minutes longer."

RALPH WALDO EMERSON

You always hear the usual stories of pennies on the sidewalk being good luck, gifts from angels, etc. This is the first time I've ever heard this twist on the story. Gives you something to think about.

Several years ago, a friend of mine and her husband were invited to spend the weekend at the husband's employer's home. My friend, Arlene, was nervous about the weekend. The boss was very wealthy, with a fine home on the waterway, and cars costing more than her house.

The first day and evening went well, and Arlene was delighted to have this rare glimpse into how the very wealthy live. The husband's employer was quite generous as a host, and took them to the finest restaurants. Arlene knew she would never have the opportunity to indulge in this kind of extravagance again, so was enjoying herself immensely.

As the three of them w ere about to enter an exclusive restaurant that evening, the boss was walking slightly ahead of Arlene and her husband.

He stopped suddenly, looking down on the pavement for a long, silent moment.

Arlene wondered if she was supposed to pass him. There was nothing on the ground except a single darkened penny that someone had dropped, and a few cigarette butts Still silent, the man reached down and picked up the penny.

He held it up and smiled, then put it in his pocket as if he had found a great treasure. How absurd! What need did this man have for a single penny? Why would he even take the time to stop and pick it up?

Throughout dinner, the entire scene nagged at her. Finally, she could stand it no longer. She casually mentioned that her daughter once had a coin collection, and asked if the penny he had found had been of some value .

A smile crept across the man's face as he reached into his pocket

NOTES

Every evening I turn my worries over to God. He's going to be up all night anyway!!

for the penny and held it out for her to see. She had seen many pennies before! What was the point of this?

"Look at it." He said. "Read what it says."
She read the words "United States of America "
"No, not that; read further."
"One cent?" "No, keep reading."
"In God we Trust?" "Yes!" "And?"
"And if I trust in God, the name of God is holy, even on a coin. Whenever I find a coin I see that inscription. It is written on every single United States coin, but we never seem to notice it! God drops a message right in front of me telling me to trust Him? Who am I to pass it by? When I see a coin, I pray, I stop to see if my trust IS in God at that moment. I pick the coin up as a response to God; that I do trust in Him. For a short time, at least, I cherish it as if it were gold.
I think it is God's way of starting a conversation with me. Lucky for me, God is patient and pennies are plentiful !

When I was out shopping today, I found a penny on the sidewalk. I stopped and picked it up, and realized that I had been worrying and fretting in my mind about things I cannot change. I read the words, "In God We Trust," and had to laugh. Yes, God, I get the message.

It seems that I have been finding an inordinate number of pennies in the last few months, but then, pennies are plentiful! And, God is patient...

"The Clothesline Said So Much"

A clothes line was a news forecast
To neighbors passing by.
There were no secrets you could keep
When clothes were hung to dry.

It also was a friendly link
For neighbors always knew
If company had stopped on by
To spend a night or two.

For then you'd see the 'fancy sheets'
And towels upon the line;
You'd see the 'company table cloths'
With intricate design.

The line announced a baby's birth
To folks who lived inside
As brand new infant clothes were hung
So carefully with pride.

The ages of the children could
So readily be known
By watching how the sizes changed
You'd know how much they'd grown.

It also told when illness struck,
As extra sheets were hung;
Then nightclothes, and a bathrobe, too,
Haphazardly were strung.

It said, 'Gone on vacation now'
When lines hung limp and bare.
It told, 'We're back!' when full lines sagged
With not an inch to spare.

New folks in town were scorned upon
If wash was dingy gray,
As neighbors carefully raised their brows,
And looked the other way.

But clotheslines now are of the past
For dryers make work less.
Now what goes on inside a home
Is anybody's guess.

I really miss that way of life.
It was a friendly sign
When neighbors knew each other best
By what hung on the line!

MARILYN K. WALKER

*O*nce upon a time there was a child ready to be born. So one day it asks God,"They tell me you are sending me to earth tomorrow but how am I going to live there being so small and helpless?"

God replied, "Among the many angels, I chose one just for you. She will be waiting for you and will take good care of you".

"But tell me, here in heaven, I don't do anything else but smile and sing,

that's enough for me to be happy."

God said, "Your angel will sing for you and will also smile every day.

And you will feel your angel's love and be happy."

"And how am I going to be able to understand when people talk to me,

if I don't know the language that men talk?"

God said, "Your angel will tell you the most beautiful and sweet words

you will ever hear and with much patience and care, your angel will teach you how to speak."

"And what am I going to do when I want to talk to you?"

God said, "Your angel will place your hands together and will teach you how to pray."

"I've heard that on earth there are bad men, who will protect me?"

God said, "Your angel will defend you even if it means risking it's life."

"But I will always be sad because I will not see you anymore."

God said, "Your angel will always talk to you about me and will teach you the way for you to come back to me, even though I will always be next to you."

At that moment there was much peace in Heaven, but voices from earth

could already be heard, and the child in a hurry asked softly,

"Oh God, if I am about to leave now, please tell me my angel's name."

God silenced all fear when He said, "your angel's name is of no importance."

"You will simply call her 'Mommy'."

A boy's best friend is his mother.
JOSEPH STEFANO

A little girl, asked where her home was, replied, "where mother is."
KEITH L. BROOKS

A man loves his sweetheart the most, his wife the best, but his mother the longest.
IRISH PROVERB

A mother holds her children's hands for a while...their hearts forever.

A mother is a person who seeing there are only four pieces of pie for five people, promptly announces she never did care for pie.
TENNEVA JORDAN

A mother understands what a child does not say.
JEWISH PROVERB

A mother's arms are made of tenderness and children sleep soundly in them.
VICTOR HUGO

A mother's love for her child is like nothing else in the world. It knows no law, no pity, it dares all things and crushes down remorselessly all that stands in its path.
AGATHA CHRISTIE

The House Of Happiness

Take what god gives, oh heart of mine,
And build your house of happiness.
Perchance some have been given less.
The treasure lying at your feet,
Whose value you but faintly guess,
Another builder, looking on,
Would barter Heaven to possess,

Have you found work that you can do?
Is there a heart that loves you best?
Is there a spot somewhere called home,
Where, spent and worn, your soul may rest?
A friendly tree? A book ? A song?
A dog that loves your hand's caress?
A store of health to meet life's needs?
Oh, build your house of happiness!

Trust not to to-morrow's dawn to bring
The dreamed-of joy for which you want;
You have enough of pleasant things
To house your soul in goodly state;
To-morrow time's relentless stream
May bear what now you have away,
Take what god gives, oh heart, and build
Your house of happiness to-day.

Unfolding the Rose

It is only a tiny rosebud,
A flower of God's design,
But I can't unfold the petals,
With these clumsy hands of mine
The way of unfolding flowers
Is not known to such as I,
The flower God opens sweetly
In my hands would surely die.
If I can't unfold a rosebud,
this flower of God's design -
Then how can I have wisdom
to unfold this life of mine?
So I will trust him to lead me
Each moment of every day,
And I'll ask him to guide me
Each step of the way.
For the pathway before me
My heavenly Father knows,
And I'll trust him to unfold it
Just as He unfolds the rose.

Love
knows no bounds

The passengers on the bus watched sympathetically as the attractive young woman with the white cane made her way carefully up the steps. She paid the driver and, using her hands to feel the location of the seats, walked down the aisle and found the seat he'd told her was empty. Then she settled in, placed her briefcase on her lap and rested her cane against her leg.

It had been a year since Olivia, thirty-four, became blind. Due to a medical misdiagnosis she had been rendered sightless, and she was suddenly thrown into a world of darkness, anger, frustration and self-pity. Once a fiercely independent woman, Olivia now felt condemned by this terrible twist of fate to become a powerless, helpless burden on everyone around her. "How could this have happened to me?" she would plead, her heart knotted with anger.

But no matter how much she cried or ranted or prayed, she knew the painful truth her sight was never going to return. A cloud of depression hung over Olivia's once optimistic spirit. Just getting through each day was an exercise in frustration and exhaustion. And all she had to cling to was her husband John.

John was an Air Force officer and he loved Olivia with all of his heart. When she first lost her sight, he watched her sink into despair and was determined to help his wife gain the strength and confidence she needed to become independent again. John's military background had trained him well to deal with sensitive situations, and yet he knew this was the most difficult battle he would ever face.

Finally, Olivia felt ready to return to her job, but how would she get there? She used to take the bus, but was now too frightened to get around the city by herself. John volunteered to drive her to work each day, even though they worked at opposite ends of the city.

At first, this comforted Olivia and fulfilled John's need to protect his sightless wife who was so insecure about performing the slightest task. Soon, however, John realized that this arrangement wasn't working - it was hectic, and costly. Olivia is going to have to start taking the bus again, he admitted to himself. But just the thought of mentioning it to her made him cringe. She was still so fragile, so angry. How would she react?

Just as John predicted, Olivia was horrified at the idea of taking the bus again. "I'm blind!" she responded bitterly. "How am I supposed to know where I'm going? I feel like you're abandoning me."

John's heart broke to hear these words, but he knew what had to be done. He promised Olivia that each morning and evening he would ride the bus with her, for as long as it took, until she got the hang of it. And that is exactly what happened.

For two solid weeks, John, military uniform and all, accompanied Olivia to and from work each day. He taught her how to rely on her other senses, specifically her hearing, to determine where she was and how to adapt to her new environment. He helped her befriend the bus drivers who could watch out for her, and save her a seat. He made her laugh, even on those not-so-good days when she would trip exiting the bus, or drop her briefcase.

Each morning they made the journey together, and John would take a cab back to his office. Although this routine was even more costly and exhausting than the previous one, John knew it was only a matter of time before Olivia would be able to ride the bus on her own. He believed in her, in the Olivia he used to know before she'd lost her sight, who wasn't afraid of any challenge and who would never, ever quit.

Finally, Olivia decided that she was ready to try the trip on her own. Monday morning arrived, and before she left, she threw her arms around John, her temporary bus riding companion, her husband, and her best friend.

Her eyes filled with tears of gratitude for his loyalty, his patience, his love. She said good-bye, and for the first time, they went their separate ways. Monday, Tuesday, Wednesday, Thursday... Each day on her own went perfectly, and Olivia had never felt better. She was doing it! She was going to work all by herself!

On Friday morning, Olivia took the bus to work as usual. As she was paying for her fare to exit the bus, the driver said, "Boy, I sure envy you." Olivia wasn't sure if the driver was speaking to her or not. After all, who on earth would ever envy a blind woman who had struggled just to find the courage to live for the past year?

Curious, she asked the driver, "Why do you say that you envy me?" The driver responded, "It must feel so good to be taken care of and protected like you are." Olivia had no idea what the driver was talking about, and asked again, "What do you mean?"
The driver answered, "You know, every morning for the past week, a fine looking gentleman in a military uniform has been standing across the corner watching you when you get off the bus. He makes sure you cross the street safely and he watches you until you enter your office building. Then he blows you a kiss, gives you a little salute and walks away. You are one lucky lady."

Tears of happiness poured down Olivia's cheeks. For although she couldn't physically see him, she had always felt John's presence. She was lucky, so lucky, for he had given her a gift more powerful than sight, a gift she didn't need to see to believe - the gift of love that can bring light where there had been darkness.

I would be true, for there are those who trust me;
I would be pure, for there are those who care;
I would be strong, for there is much to suffer;
I would be brave, for there is much to dare.
I would be friend of all—the foe, the friendless;
I would be giving, and forget the gift;
I would be humble, for I know my weakness;
I would look up, and laugh, and love, and lift.

Written around 1906, this beautiful hymn by
Howard A Walter is sung in countless churches
in America.
It teaches us about truth, because by being truthful
makes people trust us.
It teaches us to be pure, because it makes people
care for us.
It teaches us to be strong, so we can help those that
are suffering.
It teaches us to be brave, for the many challenges
of life.
It teaches us friendship, so we can eliminate our
enemies with our friendliness.
It teaches us the art of giving without wanting
to be acknowledged.
It teaches us humility so we can understand the
greatness of God.
It teaches us to look up to receive God's help.
It teaches us to be of a cheerful spirit to lighten
the burdens of others.
It teaches us that love is the answer to life's troubles.
It teaches us to be God's instruments and lift the
down-trodden.
Let us then look up, & laugh, and love and lift.

Yuva

YESTERDAY, TODAY, TOMORROW

There are two days in every week
about which we should not worry.
Two days which should be kept free
from fear and apprehension.
One of these days is yesterday with its mistakes and cares,
Its faults and blunders, its aches and pains.
Yesterday has passed forever beyond our control.
All the money in the world cannot bring back yesterday.
We cannot undo a single act we performed.
We cannot erase a single word we said. Yesterday is gone.
The other day we should not worry about is tomorrow.
With its possible adversities, its burdens,
Its large promise and poor performance.
Tomorrow is also beyond our immediate control.
Tomorrow's Sun will rise, either in splendor
or behind a mask of clouds, but it will rise.
Until it does, we have no stake in tomorrow,
for it is yet unborn.
This just leaves only one day . . . Today.
Any person can fight the battles of just one day.
It is only when you and I add the burdens of
those two awful eternity's - yesterday and tomorrow
that we break down.
It is not the experience of today that drives people mad.
It is the remorse or bitterness for something
which happened yesterday and
the dread of what tomorrow may bring.
Let us therefore live but one day at a time.

POSSIBLE AUTHOR JENNIFER KRITSCH

The choice is yours

There once was an oyster
Whose story I tell,
Who found that some sand
Had got into his shell.

It was only a grain,
but it gave him great pain.
For oysters have feelings
Although they're so plain.

Now, did he berate
the harsh workings of fate
That had brought him
To such a deplorable state?

Did he curse at the government,
Cry for election,
And claim that the sea should
Have given him protection?

'No,' he said to himself
As he lay on a shell,
Since I cannot remove it,
I shall try to improve it.

Now the years have rolled around,
As the years always do,
And he came to his ultimate
Destiny stew.

And the small grain of sand
That had bothered him so
Was a beautiful pearl
All richly aglow.

Now the tale has a moral,
for isn't it grand
What an oyster can do
With a morsel of sand?

What couldn't we do
If we'd only begin
With some of the things
That get under our skin.

The best day of my Life

Today, when I awoke, I suddenly realized that this is the best day of my life, ever!

There were times when I wondered if I would make it to today, but I did! And because I did I'm going to celebrate!

Today, I'm going to celebrate what an unbelievable life I have had so far: the accomplishments, the many blessings, and, yes, even the hardships because they have served to make me stronger.

I will go through this day with my head held high, and a happy heart.

I will marvel at God's seemingly simple gifts: the morning dew, the sun, the clouds, the trees, the flowers, and the birds. Today, none of these,miraculous creations will escape my notice.

Today, I will share my excitement for life with other people. I'll make someone smile. I'll go out of my way to perform an unexpected act of kindness for someone I don't even know.

Today, I'll give a sincere compliment to someone who seems down.

I'll tell a child how special he is, and I'll tell someone I love just how deeply I care for them and how much they mean to me.
Today is the day I quit worrying about what I don't have and start being grateful for all the wonderful things God has already given me.

I'll remember that to worry is just a waste of time because my faith in God and his Divine Plan ensures everything will be just fine.
Tonight, before I go to bed, I'll go outside and raise my eyes to the heavens. I will stand in awe at the beauty of the stars and the moon, and I will praise God for these magnificent treasures.
As the day ends and I lay my head down on my pillow, I will thank the Almighty for the best day of my life. And I will sleep the sleep of a contented child, excited with expectation because I know tomorrow is going to be ... The Best Day Of My Life!

Ah! There is nothing like staying at home, for real comfort."
JANE AUSTEN

A stranger passed by

I ran into a stranger as he passed by, "Oh, excuse me please"
was my reply.
He said, "Please excuse me too; Wasn't even watching for you."

We were very polite, this stranger and I.
We went on our way and we said good-bye.
But at home a different story is told,
How we treat our loved ones, young and old.
Later that day, cooking the evening meal,
My daughter stood beside me very still.
When I turned, I nearly knocked her down.
"Move out of the way," I said with a frown.
She walked away, her little heart was broken.
I didn't realize how harshly I'd spoken.

While I lay awake in bed,
God's still small voice came to me and said,
"While dealing with a stranger, common courtesy you use,
But the children you love, you seem to abuse.

Look on the kitchen floor,
You'll find some flowers there by the door.
Those are the flowers she brought for you.
She picked them herself: pink, yellow and blue.
She stood quietly not to spoil the surprise,
and you never saw the tears in her eyes."

By this time, I felt very small, and now my tears began to fall.
I quietly went and knelt by her bed;
"Wake up, little girl, wake up," I said.
"Are these the flowers you picked for me?"
She smiled, "I found 'em, out by the tree.
I picked 'em because they're pretty like you.
I knew you'd like 'em, especially the blue."

I said, "Daughter, I'm sorry for the way I acted today;
I shouldn't have yelled at you that way."

She said, "Oh, Mom, that's okay. I love you anyway."
I said, "Daughter, I love you too, and I do like the flowers, especially the blue."

Are you aware that: If we die tomorrow, the company that we are working for could easily replace us in a matter of days. But the family we left behind will feel the loss for the rest of their lives. And come to think of it, we pour ourselves more into work than to our family --an unwise investment indeed. That's why dear friends, as I have myself learnt, how words said in a rude way, can hurt someone, it's better to speak nicely, and with gentleness, especially when the situation is difficult and everyone is tense.

Fear knocked at the door.
Faith answered.
No one was there.
OLD ENGLISH LEGEND

Faith is the daring of the soul to
go farther than it can see.
WILLIAM NEWTON CLARK

The best help is not to bear the
troubles of others for them, but
to inspire them with the courage
and energy to bear their burdens
for themselves and meet the dif-
ficulties of life bravely.
JOHN LUBBOCK

Every man should keep a fair-
sized cemetery in which to bury
the faults of his friends.
HENRY WARD BEECHER

O lord, that lends me life,
lend me a heart
replete with thankfulness.
SHAKESPEARE

For flowers that bloom
about our feet;
For tender grass
so fresh and sweet;
For song of bird and
hum of bee;
For all things fair
we hear and see,
Father in Heaven,
we thank Thee!
RALPH WALDO EMERSON

Into the well which supplies
thee with water, cast no stones.
THE TALMUD

It was probably a mistake to
pursue happiness; much better
to create happiness; still better
to create happiness for others.
The more happiness
you created for others
the more would be yours-
a solid satisfaction that no one
could ever take away from you.
LLOYD DOUGLAS

A Kindergarten teacher was observing her classroom of chil-
dren while they drew. She would occasionally walk around to see
each child's work.
As she got to one little girl who was working diligently, she
asked what the drawing was? The girl replied, "I'm drawing God."
The teacher paused and said, "But no one knows what God looks
like." Without missing a beat, or looking up from her drawing,
the girl replied, "They will in a minute."

Lord make me a channel of Thy peace,

That where there is hatred I may bring love,

That where there is wrong I may bring the spirit of forgiveness.

That where there is discord I may bring harmony,

That where there is error I may bring truth,

That where there is doubt I may bring faith,

That where there is despair I may bring hope

That where there are shadows I may bring thy light,

That where there is sadness I may bring joy.

Lord, grant that I may seek rather to comfort than to be comforted;

To understand than to be understood;

To love than to be loved;

For it is by giving that one receives;

It is by self-forgetting that one finds;

It is by forgiving that one is forgiven;

It is by dying that one awakens to eternal life.

ST. FRANCIS OF ASSISI

 *John Blanchard* stood up from the bench, straightened his Army uniform, and studied the crowd of people making their way through Grand Central Station.

He looked for the girl whose heart he knew, but whose face he didn't, the girl with the rose. His interest in her had begun thirteen months before in a Florida library. Taking a book off the shelf he found himself intrigued, not with the words of the book, but with the notes penciled in the margin. The soft handwriting reflected a thoughtful soul and insightful mind.

In the front of the book, he discovered the previous owner's name, Miss Hollis Maynell. With time and effort he located her address. She lived in New York City. He wrote her a letter introducing himself and inviting her to correspond. The next day he was shipped overseas for service in World War II.

During the next year and one-month the two grew to know each other through the mail. Each letter was a seed falling on a fertile heart. A Romance was budding. Blanchard requested a photograph, but she refused. She felt that if he really cared, it wouldn't matter what she looked like.

When the day finally came for him to return from Europe, they scheduled their first meeting - 7:00 PM at the Grand Central Station in New York.

"You'll recognize me," she wrote, "by the red rose I'll be wearing on my lapel."

So at 7:00 he was in the station looking for a girl whose heart he loved, but whose face he'd never seen.

I'll let Mr. Blanchard tell you what happened:

A young woman was coming toward me, her figure long and slim. Her blonde hair lay back in curls from her delicate ears; her eyes were blue as flowers. Her lips and chin had a gentle firmness, and in her pale green suit she was like springtime come alive.

I started toward her, entirely forgetting to notice that she was not wearing a rose. As I moved, a small, provocative smile curved her lips. "Going my way, sailor?" she murmured.

Almost uncontrollably I made one step closer to her, and then I saw Hollis Maynell. She was standing almost directly behind the girl. A woman well past 40, she had graying hair tucked under a worn hat. She was more than plump, her thick-ankled feet thrust into low-heeled shoes. The girl in the green suit was walking quickly away.

I felt as though I was split in two, so keen was my desire to follow her, and yet so deep was my longing for the woman whose spirit had truly companioned me and upheld my own.

And there she stood. Her pale, plump face was gentle and sensible, her gray eyes had a warm and kindly twinkle. I did not hesitate. My fingers gripped the small worn blue leather copy of the book that was to identify me to her.

This would not be love, but it would be something precious, something perhaps even better than love, a friendship for which I had been and must ever be grateful. I squared my shoulders and saluted and held out the book to the woman, even though while I spoke I felt choked by the bitterness of my disappointment.

"I'm Lieutenant John Blanchard, and you must be Miss Maynell. I am so glad you could meet me; may I take you to dinner?"

The woman's face broadened into a tolerant smile.

"I don't know what this is about, son," she answered, "but the young lady in the green suit who just went by, she begged me to wear this rose on my coat. And she said if you were to ask me out to dinner, I should go and tell you that she is waiting for you in the big restaurant across the street. She said it was some kind of test!"

"How wonderful it is that nobody need wait a single moment before starting to improve the world."
ANNE FRANK

"Look up and not down. Look forward and not back. Look out and not in, and lend a hand."
EDWARD EVERETT HALE

"When you cease to make a contribution, you begin to die."
ELEANOR ROOSEVELT

"If you haven't any charity in your heart, you have the worst kind of heart trouble."
BOB HOPE

"Success has nothing to do with what you gain in life or accomplish for yourself. It's what you do for others."
DANNY THOMAS

"Blessed are those who can give without remembering and take without forgetting."
ELIZABETH BIBESCO

"The wise person understands that his own happiness must include the happiness of others."
DENNIS WEAVER

"A life isn't significant except for its impact on other lives."
JACKIE ROBINSON

Will

There is no chance, no destiny, no fate,
Can circumvent or hinder or control
The firm resolve in a determined soul.
Gifts count for nothing; will alone is great;
All things give way fore it, soon or late.
What obstacles can stay the mighty force
Of the sea-seeking river in its course,
Or cause the ascending orb of day to wait?
Each wellborn soul must win what it deserves.
Let the fool prate of luck. The fortunate
Is he whose earnest purpose never swerves,
Whose slightest action or inaction serves
The one great aim.
Why, even Death's stands still,
And waits an hour sometimes for such a will.
Ella Wheeler Wilcox

For the rise and set of the sun each day
I am thankful.

For the bounty and beauty of mother earth
I am thankful.

For the home where the heart of my family resides
I am thankful.

For the enduring devotion of steadfast friendships
I am thankful.

For the pleasure of unrestricted laughter and silly moments
I am thankful.

For the numerous shoulders that share the weight of my sorrows
I am thankful.

For the pages of memories in my book of time
I am thankful.

For all I have and all I am able to give
I am thankful.

For the setting aside of an eminent day
to gather in love, to pause and say:

"I am grateful for the abundance of blessings in my life."

I am thankful.

Two men, both seriously ill, occupied the same hospital room. One man was allowed to sit up in his bed for an hour each afternoon to help drain the fluid from his lungs. His bed was next to the room's only window. The other man had to spend all his time flat on his back.

The men talked for hours on end. They spoke of their wives and families, their homes, their jobs, their involvement in the military service, where they had been on vacation. And every afternoon when the man in the bed by the window could sit up, he would pass the time by describing to his roommate all the things he could see outside the window.

The man in the other bed began to live for those one-hour periods where his world would be broadened and enlivened by all the activity and color of the world outside.

The window overlooked a park with a lovely lake. Ducks and swans played on the water while children sailed their model boats. Young lovers walked arm in arm amidst flowers of every color of the rainbow. Grand old trees graced the landscape, and a fine view of the city skyline could be seen in the distance.

As the man by the window described all this in exquisite detail, the man on the other side of the room would close his eyes and imagine the picturesque scene. One warm afternoon the man by the window described a parade passing by. Although the other man couldn't hear the band - he could see it in his mind's eye as the gentleman by the window portrayed it with descriptive words. Days and weeks passed.

One morning, the day nurse arrived to bring water for their baths only to find the lifeless body of the man by the window, who had died peacefully in his sleep. She was saddened and called the hospital attendants to take the body away.

As soon as it seemed appropriate, the other man asked if he could be moved next to the window. The nurse was happy to make the switch, and after making sure he was comfortable, she left him alone. Slowly, painfully, he propped himself up on one elbow to take his first look at the world outside. Finally, he would have the joy of seeing it for himself.

He strained to slowly turn to look out the window beside the bed. It faced a blank wall. The man asked the nurse what could have compelled his deceased roommate who had described such wonderful things outside this window.
The nurse responded that the man was blind and could not even see the wall. She said, "Perhaps he just wanted to encourage you."

Epilogue. . . .There is tremendous happiness in making others happy, despite our own situations. Shared grief is half the sorrow, but happiness when shared, is doubled. If you want to feel rich, just count all of the things you have that money can't buy. "Today is a gift, that's why it is called the present."

Our heroes

Here's a hand to the boy who has courage

To do what he knows to be right;

When he falls in the way of temptation,

He has a hard battle to fight.

Who strives against self and his comrades

Will find a most powerful foe.

All honor to him if he conquers.

A cheer for the boy who says 'No!"

Tbere's many a battle fought daily

The world knows nothing about;

There's many a brave little soldier

Whose strength puts a legion to rout.

And he who fights sin singlehanded

Is more of a hero, I say,

Than he who leads soldiers to battle

And conquers by arms in the fray.

Be steadfast, my boy, when you're tempted,

To do what you know to be right.

Stand firm by the colors of manhood,

And you will o'ercome in the fight.

"The right," be your battle cry ever

In waging the warfare of life,

And God, who knows who are the heroes,

Will give you the strength for the strife.

PHOEBE CARY

Imagine there is a bank that credits your account each morning with $86,400. It carries over no balance from day to day. Every evening deletes whatever part of the balance you failed to use during the day.

What would you do? Draw out every cent, of course!!!! Each of us has such a bank. Its name is TIME.

Every morning, it credits you with 86,400 seconds. Every night it writes off, as lost, whatever of this you have failed to invest to good purpose. It carries over no balance. It allows no overdraft. Each day it opens a new account for you. Each night it burns the remains of the day. If you fail to use the day's deposits, the loss is yours.

There is no going back. There is no drawing against the "tomorrow". You must live in the present on today's deposits. Invest it so as to get from it the utmost in health, happiness, and success!

The clock is running. Make the most of today.
To realize the value of ONE YEAR, ask a student who failed a grade.
To realize the value of ONE MONTH, ask a mother who gave birth to a premature baby.
To realize the value of ONE WEEK, ask the editor of a weekly newspaper.
.
To realize the value of ONE HOUR, ask the lovers who are waiting to meet.
To realize the value of ONE MINUTE, ask a person who missed the train.
To realize the value of ONE SECOND, ask a person who just avoided an accident.
To realize the value of ONE MILLISECOND, ask the person who won a silver medal in the Olympics
Treasure every moment that you have! And treasure it more because you shared it with someone special, special enough to spend your time. And remember that time waits for no one.

Ideals

Some men deem
Gold their god, and some esteem
Honor is the chief content
That to man in life is lent;
And some others do contend,
Quite none like to a friend;
Others hold there is no wealth
Compared to a perfect health;
Some man's mind in quiet stands
When he is lord of many lands;
But I did sigh, and said all this
Was but a shade of perfect bliss;
And in my thoughts I did approve
Naught so sweet as is true love.

ROBERT GREENE

The supreme happiness of life is the conviction of being loved for yourself, or, more correctly, being loved in spite of yourself.

VICTOR HUGO

Love is the enchanted dawn of every heart.

LAMARTINE

To love very much is to love inadequately. We love – that is all. Love cannot be modified without being nullified. Love is a short word but it contains everything. Love means the body, the soul, the life, the entire being. We feel love as we feel the warmth of our blood, we breathe love as we breathe the air, we hold it in ourselves as we hold our thoughts. Nothing more exists for us. Love is not a word; it is a wordless state indicated by four letters ...

GUY DE MAUPASSANT

We can read poetry,
and recite poetry,
but to live poetry
is the symphony of life.
S. FRANCIS FOOTE

If you want to keep your feet on the ground, carry some responsibilities on your shoulders.

Never does a man know the force that is in him till some mighty affection or grief has humiliated the soul.
FREDERICK W. ROBERTSON

We are all if we can remember way back when children were strong enough to walk to school.

Sorrow is a fruit: God does not make it grow on limbs too weak to bear it.
VICTOR HUGO

Love never fails;
Character never quits;
and with patience
and persistence;
dreams do come true.
PETE MARAVICH

A man may be able to trade his reputation for money, but he can't trade back.

A child is the greatest poem ever known.
CHRISTOPHER MORLEY

Here are some inspirational words I have hanging above my desk. Perhaps they might be of use to others! They coincide with a wonderful bumper sticker:

We are not human beings having spiritual experiences, we are spiritual beings having human experiences.

We eat right, we work out, our minds are finely tuned, but how many of us consider the nourishment of our souls?

We are body-mind spirit. They cannot exist separately.
If we do not nurture our complete self, we die at some level. We begin to wither with a feeling of emptiness.

A vague, persistent feeling that "something is missing." A feeling of being dead inside.
We go about our daily lives, we smile, we manage....and inside, where no one can hear, we wail. Very little in our culture is deeply meaningful, feeding our soul, taking us deeper than our shallow, homogenized living.

Indeed, living in any other way but the narrowly-prescribed cultural mode is considered strange and suspect, even if pain and suffering are a dominant part of that mode.
Yet we are meant to be joyful creatures, feeling our innate aliveness and our connectedness to the Holy, Universe and Spirit.

Of the Earth dwellers, we alone have been gifted with consciousness and free will. But how tragically we waste our precious moments.

This is your hour

This is your hour – creep on it!
Summon your power, leap on it!
Grasp it, clasp it, hold it tight!
Strike it, spite it, with full might!
If you take too long to ponder,
Opportunity may wander.
Yesterday's a bag of sorrow;
No man ever finds Tomorrow.
Hesitation is a mire –
Climb out, climb up, climb on higher!
Fumble, stumble, risk a tumble,
Make a start, however humble!
Do your best and do it now!
Pluck and grit will find out how.
Persevere, although you tire—
While a spark is left, there's fire.
Distrust doubt; doubt is a liar.
Even if all mankind jeer you,
You can force the world
to cheer you.

HERBERT KAUFMAN

A couple had two little boys, ages 8 and 10, who were excessively mischievous. They were always getting into trouble and their parents knew that, if any mischief occurred in their town, their sons were probably involved.

They boys' mother heard that a clergyman in town had been successful in disciplining children, so she asked if he would speak with her boys. The clergyman agreed, but asked to see them individually. So the mother sent her 8-year-old first, in the morning, with the older boy to see the clergyman in the afternoon.

The clergyman, a huge man with a booming voice, sat the younger boy down and asked him sternly, "Where is God?"

The boy's mouth dropped open, but he made no response, sitting there with his mouth hanging open, wide-eyed. So the clergyman repeated the question in an even sterner tone, "Where is God!!?" Again the boy made no attempt to answer. So the clergyman raised his voice even more and shook his finger in the boy's face and bellowed, "WHERE IS GOD!?"

The boy screamed and bolted from the room, ran directly home and dove into his closet, slamming the door behind him. When his older brother found him in the closet, he asked, "What happened?"

The youngest brother gasped for breath and replied, "We are in BIG trouble this time dude. God is missing and they think WE did it!"

Life is the greatest of all bargains;
you get it for nothing.
YIDDISH SAYING

Procrastination

He was going to be all that a mortal could be
Tomorrow;
No one should be kinder nor braver than he
Tomorrow;
A friend who was troubled and weary he knew
Who'd be glad of a lift and who needed it, too;
On him he would call and see what he could do
Tomorrow.
Each morning he stacked up the letters he'd write
Tomorrow;
And he thought of the folks he would fill with delight
Tomorrow;
It was too bad, indeed, he was busy today,
And hadn't a minute to stop on his way;
"More time I'll have to give others," he'd say
"Tomorrow."
The greatest of workers this man would have been
Tomorrow;
But the fact is he died, and he faded from view,
And all that he life here when living was through
Was a mountain of things he intended to do
Tomorrow.

Once when I was a teenager, my father and I were standing in line to buy tickets for the circus. Finally, there was only one family between us and the ticket counter.

This family made a big impression on me. There were eight children, all probably under the age of 12. You could tell they didn't have a lot of money. Their clothes were not expensive, but they were clean.

The children were well-behaved, all of them standing in line, two-by-two behind their parents, holding hands. They were excitedly jabbering about the clowns, elephants and other acts they would see that night. One could sense they had never been to the circus before. It promised to be a highlight of their young lives. The father and mother were at the head of the pack standing proud as could be. The mother was holding her husband's hand, looking up at him as if to say, "You're my knight in shining armor." He was smiling and basking in pride, looking at her as if to reply, "You got that right."

The ticket lady asked the father how many tickets he wanted. He proudly responded, "Please let me buy eight children's tickets and two adult tickets so I can take my family to the circus."

The ticket lady quoted the price. The man's wife let go of his hand, her head dropped, the man's lip began to quiver. The father leaned a little closer and asked, "How much did you say?"

The ticket lady again quoted the price. The man didn't have enough money.
How was he supposed to turn and tell his eight kids that he didn't have enough money to take them to the circus?

Seeing what was going on, my dad put his hand into his pocket, pulled out a $20 bill and dropped it on the ground. (We were not wealthy in any sense of the word!) My father reached down, picked up the bill, tapped the man on the shoulder and said, "Excuse me, sir, this fell out of your pocket."

The man knew what was going on. He wasn't begging for a handout but certainly appreciated the help in a desperate, heartbreaking, embarrassing situation. He looked straight into my dad's eyes, took my dad's hand in both of his, squeezed tightly onto the $20 bill, and with his lip quivering and a tear streaming down his cheek, he replied, "Thank you, thank you, sir. This really means a lot to me and my family."

My father and I went back to our car and drove home. We didn't go to the circus that night, but we didn't go without.

EVER WONDER ...

Why the sun lightens our hair, but darkens our skin?

Why women can't put on mascara with their mouth closed?

Why don't you ever see the headline Psychic Wins Lottery'?

Why is 'abbreviated' such a long word?

Why is it that doctors call what they do 'practice'?

Why is lemon juice made with artificial flavor, and dish washing liquid made with real lemons?

Why is the man who invests all your money called a broker?

Why is the time of day with the slowest traffic called rush hour?

Why isn't there mouse-flavored cat food?

You know that indestructible black box that is used on airplanes? Why don't they make the whole plane out of that stuff?!

Why are they called apartments when they are all stuck together?

If con is the opposite of pro, is Congress the opposite of progress?

If flying is so safe, why do they call the airport the terminal?

Whatever task that you undertake, do it with all your heart and soul. Always be courteous, never be discouraged. Beware of him who promises something for nothing. Do not blame anybody for your mistakes and failures. Do not look for approval except in the consciousness of doing your best.

BERNARD M. BARUCH

I will govern my life and thoughts as if the whole world were to see the one and read the other, for what does it signify to make anything a secret to my neighbor, when to God, who is the searcher of our hearts, all our privacies are open?

SENECA

The holiest of all holidays are those Kept by ourselves in silence and apart, The secret anniversaries of the heart...

HENRY WADSWORTH LONGFELLOW

If you begin the day with love in your heart, peace in your nerves, and truth in your mind, you not only benefit by their presence but also bring them to others, to your family and friends, and to all those whose destiny draws across your path that day.

He who aspires

That low man seeks a little thing to do,
Sees it and does it;
This high man, with a great thing to pursue,
Dies ere he knows it.
That low man goes on adding one to one,—
His hundred's soon hit;
This high man, aiming at a million,
Misses an unit.
That has the world here—should he need the next,
Let the world mind him!
This throws himself on God, and unperplexed
Seeking shall find him.

ROBERT BROWNING

The teacher said, "I'll give $20 to the child who can tell me who was the most famous man who ever lived."

An Irish boy put his hand up and said, "It was St. Patrick." The teacher said, "Sorry Sean, that's not correct."

Then a French boy put his hand up and said, "It was Napoleon." The teacher replied, "I'm sorry, Pierre, that's not right either."

Finally, a Jewish boy raised his hand and said, "It was Jesus Christ." The teacher said, "That's absolutely right, Daniel, come up here and I'll give you the $20."

As the teacher was giving Daniel his money, she said, "You know Daniel, you being Jewish, I was very surprised you said Jesus Christ." Daniel replied, "Yeah. In my heart I knew it was Moses, but business is business."

How much does a miracle cost?

*T*ess was a precocious eight year old when she heard her Mom and Dad talking about her little brother, Andrew. All she knew was that he was very sick and they were completely out of money. They were moving to an apartment complex next month because Daddy didn't have the money for the doctor bills and our house. Only a very costly surgery could save him now and it was looking like there was noone to loan them the money. She heard Daddy say to her tearful Mother with whispered desperation, "Only a miracle can save him now."

Tess went to her bedroom and pulled a glass jelly jar from its hiding place in the closet. She poured all the change out on the floor and counted it carefully. Three times, even. The total had to be exactly perfect. No chance here for mistakes. Carefully placing the coins back in the jar and twisting on the cap, she slipped out the back door and made her way 6 blocks to Rexall's Drug Store with the big red Indian Chief sign above the door.

She waited patiently for the pharmacist to give her some attention but he was too busy at this moment. Tess twisted her feet to make a scuffing noise. Nothing. She cleared her throat with the most disgusting sound she could muster. No good. Finally she took a quarter from her jar and banged it on the glass counter. That did it! "And what do you want?" the pharmacist asked in an annoyed tone of voice.

"I'm talking to my brother from Chicago whom I haven't seen in ages," he said without waiting for a reply to his question.

"Well, I want to talk to you about my brother," Tess answered back in the same annoyed tone. "He's really, really sick... and I want to buy a miracle."

"I beg your pardon?" said the pharmacist.

"His name is Andrew and he has something bad growing inside his head and my Daddy says only a miracle can save him now. So how much does a miracle cost?"

"We don't sell miracles here, little girl. I'm sorry but I can't help you, "the pharmacist said, softening a little.

"Listen, I have the money to pay for it. If it isn't enough, I will get the rest. Just tell me how much it costs."

The pharmacist's brother was a well dressed man. He stooped down and asked the little girl, "What kind of a miracle does you brother need?"

"I don't know," Tess replied with her eyes welling up. "I just know he's really sick and Mommy says he needs an operation. But my Daddy can't pay for it, so I want to use my money.

"How much do you have?" asked the man from Chicago.

"One dollar and eleven cents," Tess answered barely audibly. "And it's all the money I have, but I can get some more if I need to."

"Well, what a coincidence," smiled the man. "A dollar and eleven cents-the exact price of a miracle for little brothers." He took her money in one hand and with the other hand he grasped her mitten and said "Take me to where you live. I want to see your brother and meet your parents. Let's see if I have the kind of miracle you need."

That well dressed man was Dr. Carlton Armstrong, a surgeon, specializing in neuro-surgery. The operation was completed without charge and it wasn't long until Andrew was home again and doing well. Mom and Dad were happily talking about the chain of events that had led them to this place. "That surgery", her Mom whispered. "was a real miracle. I wonder how much it would have cost?"

Tess smiled. She knew exactly how much a miracle cost... one dollar and eleven cents ...... plus the faith of a little child.

> A miracle is not the suspension of natural law,
> but the operation of a higher law.

The Prayer
of the bride

O God, I have come apart from the confusion. I want to still my soul for awhile. I want to feel the eternal and the fixed and the everlasting in this time.

God, make me a good wife. Make me a truth-seeing wife.

I have heard of many shipwrecks. Let our marriage sail safe. I have heard that two grow sometimes bitter and apart; let us never be separated in soul one from the other.

I have heard that things small and great come between husband and wife; let us stand side-by-side till death do us part. I have heard that Love grows cold; O let the fire on our hearts' hearthstone never die.

God, make me a good woman, so that my husband shall always keep that reverence for me he now has.

Make me a wise woman, that I may never sacrifice our mutual love upon the altar of any selfishness or opinion of mine. Make me wise to weigh values, and never slay the great things of life and love for the sake of any littleness.

O God, keep us together. That most of all. Let me never lose his love. Let my own heart never grow cold.

Keep my husband. Let him succeed in the things worthwhile. Give him courage. Never let that which in him now charms me fall from him. I want to love him always. Make him lovable.

God, keep me just human and companionable. Let my beloved find in me a friendship as well as love.

We shall have storms; let true love and wisdom carry us safely through. We shall have misunderstandings; let love so deep beneath them make them but surface ripples.

No matter what may happen, O God, so dispose events that we may always be each the refuge and stay of the other.

And if so be it that we live to old age, let love still abide.

I have chosen this man, O God. Make me faithful, for better, for worse, for richer, for poorer, in sickness and in health, so long as we both shall live.

Amen

FRANK CRANE IN THE LADIES' HOME JOURNAL, JUNE, 1912

A sense of a goose

Next Autumn, when you see geese heading south for the winter, flying in a "V" formation, you might consider what science has discovered as to why they fly that way. As each bird flaps its wings, it creates an uplift for the bird immediately following. By flying in a "V" formation, the whole flock adds at least 71 percent greater flying range than if each bird flew on its own.

People who share a common direction and sense of community can get where they are going more quickly and easily, because they are travelling on the thrust of one another.

When a goose falls out of formation, it suddenly feels the drag and resistance of trying to go it alone and quickly gets back into formation to take advantage of the lifting power of the bird in front.

If we have the sense of a goose, we will stay in formation with those people who are heading the same way we are.

When the head goose gets tired, it rotates back in the wing and another goose flies point.

It is sensible to take turns doing demanding jobs, whether with people or with geese flying south.

Geese honk from behind to encourage those up front to keep up their speed.

What message do we give when we honk from behind?

Finally - and this is important - when a goose gets sick or is wounded by gunshot, and falls out of the formation, two other geese fall out with that goose and follow it down to lend help and protection. They stay with the fallen goose until it is able to fly or until it dies; and only then do they launch out on their own, or with another formation to catch up with their own group.

If we have the sense of a goose, we will stand by each other like that.

There are little eyes upon you
and they're watching night and day.
There are little ears that quickly
take in every word you say.
There are little hands all eager
to do anything you do;
And a little boy who's dreaming
of the day he'll be like you.
You're the little fellow's idol,
you're the wisest of the wise.
In his little mind about you
no suspicions ever rise.
He believes in you devoutly,
holds all you say and do;
He will say and do, in your way
when he's grown up just like you.
There's a wide-eyed little fellow
who believes you're always right;
and his eyes are always opened,
and he watches day and night.
You are setting an example
every day in all you do;
For the little boy who's waiting
to grow up to be like you.

$\mathcal{A}$ great philosopher once said that it was a luxury to be understood. What a statement. Everyday in our life, we encounter differences in our opinions, that lead to arguments and loss of relationships. We loose a lot due to the disease called "misunderstanding". An Irishman by the name of Thomas Bracken once wrote:

Not understood, we move along asunder;
Our paths grow wider as the seasons creep
Along the years; we marvel and we wonder
Why life is life, and then we fall asleep
Not understood.

Not understood, we gather false impressions
And hug them closer as the years go by;
Till virtues often seem to us transgressions;
And thus men rise and fall, and live and die
Not understood.

Not understood! Poor souls with stunted vision
Oft measure giants with their narrow gauge;
The poisoned shafts of falsehood and derision
Are oft impelled 'gainst those who mould the age,
Not understood.

Not understood! The secret springs of action
Which lie beneath the surface and the show,
Are disregarded; with self-satisfaction
We judge our neighbours, and they often go
Not understood.

Not understood! How trifles often change us!
The thoughtless sentence and the fancied slight
Destroy long years of friendship, and estrange us,
And on our souls there falls a freezing blight;
Not understood.

Not understood! How many breasts are aching
For lack of sympathy! Ah! day by day
How many cheerless, lonely hearts are breaking!
How many noble spirits pass away,
Not understood.

O God! that men would see a little clearer,
Or judge less harshly where they cannot see!
O God! that men would draw a little nearer
To one another, -- they'd be nearer Thee,
And understood.

Great advice to pass on to Your daughters

1. Don't imagine you can change a man - unless he's in diapers.

2. What do you do if your boyfriend walks-out? You shut the door.

3. If they put a man on the moon - they should be able to put them all up there.

4. Never let your man's mind wander - it's too little to be out alone.

5. Go for younger men. You might as well - they never mature anyway.

6. Men are all the same - they just have different faces, so that you can tell them apart.

7. Definition of a bachelor; a man who has missed the opportunity to make some woman miserable.

8. Women don't make fools of men - most of them are the do-it-yourself types.

9. Best way to get a man to do something, is to suggest they are too old for it.

10. Love is blind, but marriage is a real eye-opener.

11. If you want a committed man, look in a mental hospital.

12. The children of Israel wandered around the desert for 40 years.
      Even in biblical times, men wouldn't ask for directions.

13. If he asks what sort of books you're interested in, tell him
    checkbooks.

14. Remember a sense of humor does not mean that you tell him
      jokes, it means that you laugh at his.

15. Sadly, all men are created equal...

*A*n elderly woman walked into the local country
church. The friendly usher greeted her at the door and
helped her up the flight of steps. "Where would you like to
sit?" he asked politely.
"The front row please." she answered.
"You really don't want to do that", the usher said, "The
pastor is really boring."
"Do you happen to know who I am?" the woman inquired.
"No." he said.
"I'm the pastor's mother," she replied indignantly.
"Do you know who I am?" he asked.
"No." she said.
"Good", he answered.

First Class Justice

Human beings have a lot of foolish pride, and there is no limit to the prejudices we have. But to be prejudiced against another human because he or she was born of a different color skin, is totally inhuman and inconsiderate. This story shows how tactfully a stewardess handled such a situation. I truly enjoyed this one and you will too.

On a British Airways flight from Johannesburg, a middle-aged, well-off South African lady has found herself sitting next to a black man. She called the cabin crew attendant over to complain about her seating.

"What seems to be the problem, Madam?" asked the attendant.

"Can't you see?" she said, "You've sat me next to a kafir. I can't possibly sit next to this disgusting human. Find me another seat!"

"Please calm down, Madam." the stewardess replied. "The flight is very full today, but I'll tell you what I'll do. I'll go and check to see if we have any seats available in club or first class".

The woman cocks a snooty look at the outraged black man beside her (not to mention many of the surrounding passengers). A few minutes later the stewardess returns with the good news, which she delivers to the lady, who cannot help but look at the people around her with a smug and self-satisfied grin.

"Madam, unfortunately, as I suspected, economy is full. I've spoken to the cabin services director, and club is also full.

However, we do have one seat in first class".

Before the lady has a chance to answer, the stewardess continues:

"It is most extraordinary to make this kind of upgrade, however, and I have had to get special permission from the captain. But, given the circumstances, the captain felt that it was outrageous that someone should be forced to sit next such an obnoxious person."

With that, she turned to the black man and said: "So if you'd like to get your things, sir, I have your seat ready for you..."

At which point, the surrounding passengers stood and gave a standing ovation while the man walked to the front of the plane.

Excuse This House

Some houses try to hide the fact
That childen shelter there –
Ours boasts of it quite openly,
The signs are every where!

For smears are on the windows,
Little smudges on the doors;
I should apologize, I guess,
For toys strewn on the floor.

But, I sat down with the children
And we played and laughed and read,
And if the door bell doesn't shine,
Their eyes will shine instead.

For when, at times, I'm forced
to choose
The one job or the other;
I want to be a housewife
But first I'll be a mother.

Life isn't about finding yourself.
Life is about creating yourself.
GEORGE BERNARD SHAW

Our lives begin to end the day
we become silent about things
that matter.
MARTIN LUTHER KING, JR.

Challenges come so we can grow
and be prepared for things we
are not equipped to handle now.
When we face our challenges
with faith, prepared to learn,
willing to make changes, and
if necessary, to let go, we are
demanding our power
be turned on.
IYANLA VANZANT

We can throw stones, complain
about them, stumble on them,
climb over them, or build with
them.
WILLIAM ARTHUR WARD

Life is a bridge. Cross over it,
but build no house on it
INDIAN PROVERB

It is wonderful how much time
good people spend fighting the
devil. If they would only expend
the same amount of energy
loving their fellow men, the devil
would die in his own tracks.
HELEN KELLER

Fold two hands together

And express a dash of sorrow
Marinate it overnight
And work on it tomorrow.
Chop one grudge in tiny pieces
Add several cups of love
Dredge with a large sized smile
Mix with the ingredients above.
Dissolve the hate within you,
By doing a good deed
Cut in and help your friend
If he should be in need.
Stir in laughter, love an kindness
From the heart it has to come,
Toss with genuine forgiveness
And give your neighbor some.
The amount of people served
Will depend on you,
It can serve the whole wide world,
If you really want it to.

If I have learned anything

I've learned that you can get by on charm for about 15 minutes.
After that, you'd better know something.

I've learned that you shouldn't compare yourself
to the best others can do, but to the best you can do.

I've learned that it's not what happens to people that's important.
It's what they do about it.

I've learned that you can do something in an instant
that will give you a heartache for life.

I've learned that no matter how thin you slice it,
there are always two sides.

I've learned that regardless of your relationship with your parents,
you miss them terribly after they die.

I've learned that it's taking me a long time
to become the person I want to be.

I've learned that it's a lot easier to react than it is to think.

I've learned that you should always leave loved ones with loving words.

It may be the last time you see them.

I've learned that you can keep going long after you think you can't.

I've learned that we are responsible for what we do,
no matter how we feel.

I've learned that either you control your attitude or it controls you.

Remember the storm is a good opportunity for the pine and the cypress to show their strength and their stability.
HO CHI MINH

In the midst of winter, I found there was, within me, an invincible summer.
ALBERT CAMUS

Where the willingness is great, the difficulties cannot be great.
MACHIAVELLI

Success and rest don't sleep together.
RUSSIAN PROVERB

Don't count the days, make the days count.
MUHAMMAD ALI

Those who wish to sing, always find a song.
SWEDISH PROVERB

Celebrate your success and find humor in your failures. Don't take yourself so seriously. Loosen up and everyone around you will loosen up. Have fun and always show enthusiasm. When all else fails, put on a costume and sing a silly song.
SAM WALTON

Throw your heart over the fence and the rest will follow.
NORMAN VINCENT PEALE

Don't make me walk when I want to fly.
GALINA DOYLA

Hold on to what is good
Even if it is a handful of earth
Hold on to what you believe in
Even if it is a tree which stands by itself
Hold on to what you must do
Even if it is a long way from here
Hold on to life
Even if it is easier to let go
Hold on to my hand
Even when I have gone away.
PUEBLO INDIAN

Maybe

Maybe God wanted us to meet the wrong people before meeting the right one so that when we finally meet the right person, we will know how to be grateful for that gift.

Maybe when the door of happiness closes, another opens, but often times we look so long at the closed door that we don't see the one which has been opened for us.

Maybe the best kind of friend is the kind you can sit on a porch and swing with, never say a word, and then walk away feeling like it was the best conversation you've ever had.

Maybe it is true that we don't know what we have got until we lose it, but it is also true that we don't know what we have been missing until it arrives.

172

"Walk a little plainer, Daddy,"
said a little boy so frail.
"I'm following in your footsteps
And I don't want to fail.
Sometimes your steps are very plain,
Sometimes they're hard to see.
So walk a little plainer, Daddy,
For you are leading me.
I know that you once walked this way
Many years ago.
And what you did along the way
I'd really like to know.
For sometimes when I'm tempted
I don't know what to do.
So, walk a little plainer, Daddy,
For I must follow you.
Someday when I am grown up,
You are like I want to be,
Then I will have a little boy,
Who will want to follow me.
And I would want to lead him right
And help him to be true.
So, walk a little plainer, Daddy,
For we must follow you.

Mother

When you were 1 year old, she fed you and bathed you.
You thanked her by crying all night long.

When you were 2 years old, she taught you to walk.
You thanked her by running away when she called.

When you were 3 years old, she made all your meals with love.
You thanked her by tossing your plate on the floor.

When you were 4 years old, she gave you some crayons
You thanked her by coloring the dining room table.

When you were 5 years old, she dressed you for the holidays.
You thanked her by plopping into the nearest pile of mud.

When you were 6 years old, she walked you to school.
You thanked her by screaming, "I'M NOT GOING!"

When you were 7 years old, she bought you a baseball.
You thanked her by throwing it through
the next-door-neighbor's window.

When you were 8 years old, she handed you an ice cream.
You thanked her by dripping it all over your lap.

When you were 9 years old, she paid for piano lessons.
You thanked her by never even bothering to practice.

When you were 10 years old she drove you all day,
from soccer to gymnastics to one birthday party after another.
You thanked her by jumping out of the car and never looking back.

When you were 11 years old, she took you and your friends
to the movies.
You thanked her by asking to sit in a different row.

When you were 12 years old, she warned you not to watch certain TV shows.
You thanked her by waiting until she left the house.

When you were 13, she suggested a haircut that was becoming.
You thanked her by telling her she had no taste.

When you were 14, she paid for a month away at summer camp.
You thanked her by forgetting to write a single letter.

When you were 15, she came home from work, looking for a hug.
You thanked her by having your bedroom door locked.

When you were 16, she taught you how to drive her car.
You thanked her by taking it every chance you could.

When you were 17, she was expecting an important call.
You thanked her by being on the phone all night.

When you were 18, she cried at your high school graduation.
You thanked her by staying out partying until dawn.

When you were 19, she paid for your college tuition, drove you to campus, carried your bags.
You thanked her by saying good-bye outside the dorm so you wouldn't be embarrassed in front of your friends.

When you were 20, she asked whether you were seeing anyone.
You thanked her by saying, "It's none of your business

When you were 21, she suggested certain careers for your future.
You thanked her by saying, "I don't want to be like you

When you were 22, she hugged you at your college graduation.
You thanked her by asking whether she could pay for a trip to Europe.

When you were 23, she gave you furniture for your first apartment.
You thanked her by telling your friends it was ugly.

When you were 24, she met your fiancé and asked about your plans for the future.
You thanked her by glaring and growling,"Muuhh-ther, please!"

When you were 25, she helped to pay for your wedding, and she cried and told you how deeply she loved you.
You thanked her by moving halfway across the country.

When you were 30, she called with some advice on the baby.
You thanked her by telling her, "Things are different now."

When you were 40, she called to remind you of a relative's birthday.
You thanked her by saying you were "really busy right now."

When you were 50, she fell ill and needed you to take care of her.
You thanked her by reading about the burden parents become to their children.

And then, one day, she quietly died.

And everything you never did, came crashing down like thunder.

IF SHE'S STILL AROUND, NEVER FORGET TO LOVE HER MORE THAN EVER

AND IF SHE'S NOT, REMEMBER HER UNCONDITIONAL LOVE.

"When you are a mother,
you are never really alone in your thoughts.
A mother always has to think twice,
once for herself and once for her child."

SOPHIA LOREN, WOMEN AND BEAUTY

177

Imagine life as a game in which you are juggling some five balls in the air. You name them – work, family, health, friends and spirit and you're keeping all of these in the air. You will soon understand that work is a rubber ball. If you drop it, it will bounce back. But the other four balls – family, health, friends and spirit are made of glass. If you drop one of these, they will be irrevocably scuffed, marked, nicked, damaged or even shattered. They will never be the same. You must understand that and strive for balance in your life. How?

Don't undermine your worth by comparing yourself with others. It is because we are different that each of us is special.

Don't set your goals by what other people deem important. Only you know what is best for you.

Don't take for granted the things closest to your heart. Cling to them as you would your life, for without them, life is meaningless.

Don't let your life slip through your fingers by living in the past or for the future. By living your life one day at a time, you live ALL the days of your life.

Don't give up when you still have something to give. Nothing is really over until the moment you stop trying.

Don't be afraid to admit that you are less than perfect. It is this fragile thread that binds us each together.

Don't be afraid to encounter risks. It is by taking chances that we learn how to be brave.

Don't shut love out of your life by saying it's impossible to find. The quickest way to receive love is to give; the fastest way to lose love is to hold it too tightly; and the best way to keep love is to give it wings.

Don't run through life so fast that you forget not only where you've been, but also where you are going.

Don't forget that a person's greatest emotional need is to feel appreciated.

Don't be afraid to learn. Knowledge is weightless, a treasure you can always carry easily.

Don't use time or words carelessly. Neither can be retrieved. Life is not a race, but a journey to be savored each step of the way.
Brian Dyson

God listens

There is this atheist swimming in the ocean. All of the sudden he sees this shark in the water, so he starts swimming towards his boat.

As he looks back he sees the shark turn and head towards him. His boat is a ways off and he starts swimming like crazy. He's scared to death, and as he turns to see the jaws of the great white beast open revealing its teeth in a horrific splendor, the atheist screams, "Oh God! Save me!"

In an instant time is frozen and a bright light shines down from above. The man is motionless in the water when he hears the voice of God say, "You are an atheist. Why do you call upon me when you do not believe in me?"

Aghast with confusion and knowing he can't lie the man replies, "Well, that's true I don't believe in you, but how about the shark? Can you make the shark believe in you?"

The Lord replies, "As you wish," and the light retracted back into the heavens and the man could feel the water begin to move once again.

As the atheist looks back he can see the jaws of the shark start to close down on him, when all of sudden the shark stops and pulls back.

Shocked, the man looks at the shark as the huge beast closes its eyes and bows its head and says, "Thank you Lord for this food for which I am about to receive..."

If it's true that girls are inclined to marry men like their fathers, it is understandable why so many mothers cry so much at weddings.

After a hard day's work at my business, I look forward to the thought of going home. One of the nicest feelings of life is to go home. A place, where we are loved inspite of ourselves, cared for and wanted. A place where someone waits for us, someone who loves us no matter what. The saying aptly says, home is where the heart is.

Going through my books, one morning I read a poem by Edwin Carlile Litsey, a banker from Kentucky during the days of world war 1. I loved the way he expressed his love for his wife, and of coming home to her. Not much is available from this very talented poet, but I will gladly share this poem with you.

When I come home, worn with the fretful day,
And find you waiting, with your smile of love,
Your arms' soft pressure all my cares remove,
Your lips strange magic all my fears allay.

When I come home – When my feet seek the shrine
Our love has builded for our worship sweet
I pass from out a world of sham and cheat
Into a tiny world of truth divine.

When I come home – it matters not how strong
The battle has beset me – in that hour
When I come home I feel your subtle power
Which flows in soothing waves, like a song.

When I come home my wonder wakes afresh
Before the mystery of your woman's way;
The skill to take and keep my hert always,
A captive thrilling in a magic mesh.

I am sure you will cherish these words of a man in love written about a hundred years ago, in the small, beautiful Marion county in Kentucky.

Yuva

The perfect partner

*Y*ears ago, I asked God to give me a spouse. "You don't own because you didn't ask" God said.

Not only I asked for a spouse but also explained what kind of spouse I wanted. I want a nice, tender, forgiving, passionate, honest, peaceful, generous, understanding, pleasant, warm, intelligent, humorous, attentive, compassionate and truthful. I even mentioned the physical characteristics I dreamt about.

As time went by I added the required list of my wanted spouse. One night, in my prayer, God talked to my heart: "My servant, I cannot give you what you want."

I asked, "Why God?" and God said "Because I am God and I am fair. God is the truth and all I do are true and right."

I asked "God, I don't understand why I cannot have what I ask from you?"

God answered, "I will explain. It is not fair and right for Me to fulfill your demand because I cannot give something that is not your own self.

It is not fair to give someone who is full of love to you if sometimes you are still hostile, or to give you someone generous but sometimes you can be cruel, or someone forgiving; however, you still hide revenge, someone sensitive; however, you are very insensitive...."

He then said to me: "It is better for Me to give you someone who I know could grow to have all qualities you are searching rather than to make you waste your time to find someone who already have the qualities you want.

Your spouse would be bone from your bone and flesh from your flesh and you will see yourself in her and both of you will be one. Marriage is like a school. It is a life-long span of education. It is where you and your partner make adjustment and aim not merely to please each other, but to be better human beings and to make a solid teamwork.

I do not give you a perfect partner, because you are not perfect either. I give you a partner with whom you would grow together"

ARE YOU THANKFUL ENOUGH?

God gave you a gift of 86,400 seconds today. Have you used one to say "thank you?"
WILLIAM A. WARD

The Pilgrims made seven times more graves than huts. No Americans have been more impoverished than these who, nevertheless, set aside a day of thanksgiving.
H.U. WESTERMAYER

Silent gratitude isn't much use to anyone.
G.B. STERN

If the only prayer you said in your whole life was, "thank you," that would suffice.
MEISTER ECKHART

There is no such thing as gratitude unexpressed. If it is unexpressed, it is plain, old-fashioned ingratitude.
ROBERT BRAULT

Gratitude is the memory of the heart.
JEAN BAPTISTE MASSIEU

When we were children we were grateful to those who filled our stockings at Christmas time. Why are we not grateful to God for filling our stockings with legs?
G.K. CHESTERTON

The only people with whom you should try to get even are those who have helped you.
JOHN E. SOUTHARD

The few

The easy roads are crowded,
And the level roads are jammed;
The pleasant little rivers
With the drifting folks are crammed.
But off yonder where it's rocky,
Where you get a better view,
You will find the ranks are thinning
And the travelers are few.

Where the going's smooth and pleasant
You will always find the throng,
For the man, more's the pity,
Seem to like to drift along.
But the steeps that call for courage,
And the task that's hard to do,
In the end result in glory
For the never-wavering few.

EDGAR A GUEST

These Days

We have taller buildings, but shorter tempers; wider freeways, but narrower viewpoints; we spend more, but have less; we buy more, but enjoy it less.

We have bigger houses and smaller families; more conveniences, but less time; we have more degrees, but less common sense; more knowledge, but less judgment; more experts, but more problems; more medicine, but less wellness.

We spend too recklessly, laugh too little, drive too fast, get too angry too quickly, stay up too late, get up too tired, read too seldom, watch TV too much, and pray too seldom.

We have multiplied our possessions, but reduced our values.

We talk too much, love too seldom and lie too often.

We've learned how to make a living, but not a life; we've added years to life, not life to years.

We've been all the way to the moon and back, but have trouble crossing the street to meet the new neighbor.

We've conquered outer space, but not inner space; we've done larger things, but not better things; we've cleaned up the air, but polluted the soul; we've split the atom, but not our prejudice; we write more, but learn less; plan more, but accomplish less.

We've learned to rush, but not to wait; we have higher incomes, but lower morals; more food but less appeasement; more acquaintances, but fewer friends; more effort but less success.

We build more computers to hold more information, to produce more copies than ever, but have less communication; we've become long on quantity, but short on quality.

These are the time of fast foods and slow digestion; tall men and short character; steep profits, and shallow relationships.

These are the times of world peace, but domestic warfare; more leisure and less fun; more kinds of food, but less nutrition.

These are days of two incomes, but more divorce; of fancier houses, but broken homes.

These are days of quick trips, disposable diapers, throwaway morality, one-night stands, overweight bodies, and pills that do everything from cheer, to quiet, to kill.

It is a time when there is much in the show window, and nothing in the stockroom.

GEORGE CARLIN

A number of frogs were traveling through the woods. Two of them fell into a deep pit. All the other frogs gathered around the pit. When they saw how deep the pit was, they told the two frogs that they were as good as dead.

The two frogs ignored the comments and tried to jump up out of the pit with all of their might. The other frogs kept telling them to stop, that they were as good as dead.

Finally, one of the frogs took heed to what the other frogs were saying and gave up. He fell down and died.

The other frog continued to jump as hard as he could. Once again, the crowd of frogs yelled at him to stop the pain and just die. He jumped even harder and finally made it out.

When he got out, the other frogs said, "Did you not hear us?" The frog explained to them that he was deaf. He thought they were encouraging him the entire time.

This story teaches two lessons:

There is the power of life and death in the tongue. An encouraging word to someone who is down can lift them up and help them make it through the day.

A destructive word to someone who is down can be the push over the edge. Be careful of what you say. Speak life to those who cross your path. Anyone can speak words that can rob another of the spirit to push forward in difficult times.

Special is the individual who will take the time to encourage another. Be kind to others.

Every evening I turn my worries over to God. He's going to be up all night anyway.

MARY C. CROWLEY

An Inspiration

However the battle is ended,
Though proudly the victor comes
With fluttering flags and prancing nags
And echoing roll of drums,
Still truth proclaims this motto,
In letters of living light –
No question is ever settled,
Until it is settled right.

Though the heel of the strong oppressor
May grind the weak to dust,
And the voices of dame with one acclaim
May call him great and just,
Let those who applaud take warning,
And keep this motto in sight –
No questions is ever settled
Until it is settled right.

Let those who have failed take courage;
Tho' the enemy seems to have won,
Tho' his ranks are strong, if he be in the wrong
The battle is not yet done;
For, as sure as the morning follows
The darkest hour of the night,
No questions is ever settled
Until it is settled right.

O man bowed down with labor!
O woman, young, yet old!
O heart oppressed in the toiler's breast
And crushed by the power of gold!
Keep on with your weary battle
Against triumphant might;
No question is ever settled
Until it is settled right.

ELLA WHEELER WILCOX

Happiness

Happiness is like a crystal,
Fair and exquisite and clear,
Broken in a million pieces,
Shattered, scattered far and near.
Now and then along life's pathway,
Lo! some shining fragments fall;
But there are so many pieces
No one ever finds them all.
You may find a bit of beauty,
Or an honest share of wealth,
While another just beside you
Gathers honor, love or health.
Vain to choose or grasp unduly,
Broken is the perfect ball;
And there are so many pieces
No one ever finds them all.
Yet the wise as on they journey
Treasure every fragment clear,
Fit them as they may together,
Imaging the shattered sphere
Learning ever to be thankful,
Though their share of it is small;
For it has so many pieces
No one ever finds them all.

PRISCILLA LEONARD

The little thing

As you might know, the head of a major company survived the tragedy of "9/11" in New York because his son started kindergarten.

Another fellow was alive because it was his turn to bring donuts.

One woman was late because her alarm clock didn't go off in time.

One was late because of being stuck on the NJ Turnpike because of an auto accident.

One of them missed his bus.

One spilled food on her clothes and had to take time to change.

One's car wouldn't start.

One went back to answer the telephone.

One had a child that dawdled and didn't get ready as soon as he should have.

One couldn't get a taxi.

The one that struck me was the man who put on a new pair of shoes that morning,

took the various means to get to work but before he got there, he developed a

blister on his foot.

He stopped at a drugstore to buy a Band-Aid. That is why he is alive today.

Now when I am stuck in traffic...

miss an elevator...

turn back to answer a ringing telephone...

all the little things that annoy me...

I think to myself...

this is exactly where God wants me to be at this very moment.

The next time your morning seems to be going wrong,

the children are slow getting dressed,

you can't seem to find the car keys,

you hit every traffic light...

don't get mad or frustrated;

God is at work watching over you.

May God continue to bless you with all those annoying little things - and may you remember and appreciate their possible purpose.

An old preacher was dying. He sent a message for his doctor and his lawyer to come to his home. When they arrived, they were ushered up to his bedroom.

As they entered the room the preacher held out his hands and motioned for them to sit, one on each side of his bed. The preacher grasped their hands, sighed contentedly, smiled and stared at the ceiling.

For a time, no one said anything. Both the doctor and lawyer were touched and flattered that the preacher would ask them to be with him during his final moments. They were also puzzled; the preacher had never given them any indication that he particularly liked either of them.

They both remembered his many long, uncomfortable sermons about greed, covetousness and avaricious behavior that made them squirm in their seats.

Finally, the doctor said, "Preacher, why did you ask us to come?

The old preacher mustered up his strength, then said weakly, "Jesus died between two thieves.. and that's how I want to go."

A man's own good breeding is the best security against other people's ill manners.
LORD CHESTERFIELD

The secret of many a man's success in the world resides in his insight into the moods of men and his tact in dealing with them.
J. G. HOLLAND

To rejoice in another's prosperity, is to give content to your own lot: to mitigate another's grief, is to alleviate or dispel your own.
THOMAS EDWARDS

Hear the meaning within the word.
WILLIAM SHAKESPEARE

Kind words are the music of the world.
F. W. FABER

We are far more liable to catch the vices than the virtues of our associates.
DENIS DIDEROT

Arguing with a fool proves there are two.
DORIS M. SMITH

Be courteous to all, but intimate with few; and let those be well-tried before you give them your confidence.
GEORGE WASHINGTON

If I have learned anything

I've learned that you should never tell a child his dreams are unlikely or outlandish. Few things are more humiliating, and what a tragedy it would be if he believed it.

I've learned that your family won't always be there for you. It may seem funny, but people you aren't related to can take care of you and love you and teach you to trust people again. Families aren't biological.

I've learned that no matter how good a friend someone is, they're going to hurt you every once in awhile and you must forgive them for that.

I've learned that it isn't always enough to be forgiven by others. Sometimes you have to learn to forgive yourself.

I've learned that no matter how bad your heart is broken, the world doesn't stop for your grief.

I've learned that our background and circumstances may have influenced who we are, but we are responsible for who we become.

I've learned that sometimes when my friends fight, I'm forced to choose sides even when I don't want to.

I've learned that just because two people argue, it doesn't mean they don't love each other.

I've learned that sometimes you have to put the individual ahead of their actions.

I've learned that it takes years to build up trust, and only seconds to destroy it.

I've learned that we don't have to change friends if we understand that friends change.

God helps

There was an old man sitting on his porch watching the rain fall. Pretty soon the water was coming over the porch and into the house.

The old man was still sitting there when a rescue boat came and the people on board said, "You can't stay here you have to come with us."

The old man replied, "No, God will save me." So the boat left. A little while later the water was up to the second floor, and another rescue boat came, and again told the old man he had to come with them.

The old man again replied, "God will save me." So the boat left him again.

An hour later the water was up to the roof and a third rescue boat approached the old man, and tried to get him to come with them.

Again the old man refused to leave stating that, "God will save him." So the boat left him again.

Soon after, the man drowns and goes to heaven, and when he sees God he asks him, "Why didn't you save me?"

God replied, "You dummy! I tried. I sent three boats after you!!"

A friend is someone
who knows the song in your heart,
and can sing it back to you
when you have forgotten the words.

DONNA ROBERTS

Three friends die in a car accident and they go to an orientation in heaven. They are all asked, "When you are in your casket and friends and family are talking about you, what would you like them to say?

The first guy says, "I would like to hear them say that I was a great doctor of my time, and a great family man."

The second guy says, "I would like to hear that I was a wonderful husband and school teacher which made a huge difference in our children of tomorrow."

The last guy replies, "I would like to hear them say ...
Look, He's moving".

When one door closes another opens. But often we look so long so regretfully upon the closed door that we fail to see the one that has opened for us.

HELEN KELLER

Any fool can count the seeds in an apple. Only God can count all the apples in one seed.
ROBERT H. SCHULLER

A brook would lose its song if God removed the rocks.

I cannot imagine how the clockwork of the universe can exist without a clockmaker.
VOLTAIRE

A person, whose Bible is falling apart, usually isn't.

A little faith will bring your soul to heaven, but a lot of faith will bring heaven to your soul.

Prayer should be our first resource not our last resort.

What we usually pray to God is not that His will be done, but that He approve ours.
HELGA BERGOLD

What the caterpillar calls the end of the world the master calls a butterfly.
RICHARD BACH

196

Are you listening?

Back when the telegraph was the was the fastest method of long-distance communication, a young man applied for a job as a Morse Code operator.

Answering an ad in the newspaper, he went to the office address that was listed. When he arrived, he entered a large, busy office filled with noise and clatter, including the sound of the telegraph in the background. A sign on the receptionist's counter instructed job applicants to fill out a form and wait until they were summoned to enter the inner office. The young man filled out his form and sat down with the seven other applicants in the waiting area. After a few minutes, the young man stood up, crossed the room to the door of the inner office, and walked right in. Naturally the other applicants perked up, wondering what was going on. They muttered among themselves that they hadn't heard any summons yet. They assumed that the young man who went into the office made a mistake and would be disqualified.

Within a few minutes, however, the employer escorted the young man out of the office and said to the other applicants, "Gentlemen, thank you very much for coming, but the job has just been filled." The other applicants began grumbling to each other, and one spoke up saying, "Wait a minute, I don't understand. He was the last to come in, and we never even got a chance to be interviewed. Yet he got the job. That's not fair!"

The employer said, "I'm sorry, but all the time you've been sitting here, the telegraph has been ticking out the following message in Morse Code: 'If you understand this message, then come right in. The job is yours.' None of you heard it or understood it. This young man did. The job is his."

We live in a world that is full of busyness and clatter, like that office. People are distracted and unable to hear the still, small voice of God as He still speaks to us. Are you tuned in to God's voice? Do you hear Him when He speaks to you? Are you listening?

The silver lining

There's never a day so sunny
But a little cloud appears;
There's never a life so happy
But has its time of tears.
Yet the sun shines out the brighter
Whenever the tempest clears.

There's never a garden growing,
With roses in every plot;
There's never a heart so hardened
But it has one tender spot.
We have only to prune the border
To find the forget-me-knot.

There's never a sun that rises
But we know 'twill set at night;
The tints that gleam in the morning
At evening are just as bright.
And that hour that is the sweetest
Is between the dark and light.

There's never a dream so happy
But the wakening makes us sad;
There's never a dream of sorrow
But the wakening makes us glad.
We shall look some day with wonder
At the trouble we have had.

TAKING LIFE FOR GRANTED

Last week, my cell phone got stolen. I lost two years of memorable messages sent by people who love me and care for me. I was hurt that there was no way I could retrieve them.

But, this incident taught me a valuable lesson. 25 years ago, when I arrived in New York, I did not have a cell phone, nor did I know the concept of one. But time brings new inventions, many of which become an important part of our life. I felt lost without my phone. I felt something missing from my day-to-day life. But it was only a cell phone. We spend our years running after things and gathering material possessions that we loose track of things we cannot replace:

Time spent with our parents
Time spent with our children
Time spent with our loved ones.

These times cannot be measured or gotten back. As a teenager, I found every opportunity to spend with my friends, that when my dad wanted to take me out, I made every excuse not to go with him. I surely regret it now, because I am in New York, thousands of miles away from him, and since his injury last year, I feel so sad that I wasted away the years when I could have had gotten so much more joy being with him.

Let this be a lesson, that people you love and those that love you, are irreplaceable, and every moment spent with them, is like being in divine presence, because caring love is the greatest of all feelings.

Yuva
(Written on April 29, 2009)

It is undeniable that the great quest of humanity is happiness. But as the world created to be happy? How many are truly happy? I've studied people in all classes and conditions, and everywhere I have found, when you get below the surface, that it is mostly the insincere individual who says, "I am happy." Nearly everybody wants something he hasn't got, and as things are constructed, what he wants is money – more money than he has in his pocket.

But after all, money can buy only a few things. Why should any one envy that captains of industry? Their lives are made up of those vast, incessant worries from which the average individual is happily spared. Worry, worry, that is the evil of life.

What do I consider the nearest approximation to happiness of which the present human is capable? Why, living on a farm which is one's own, far from the hectic, artificial conditions of the city – a farm where one gets directly from one's own soil what one needs to sustain life, with a garden in front and a healthy, normal family to contribute those small domestic joys which relieve a man from business strain.

THOMAS EDISON

The man for me

The kind of a man
for you and me!
He faces the world
unflinchingly,
And smiles as long as
the wrong exist,
With a knuckled faith
and for like fist;
He lives the life
he is preaching of,
And loves where most
is the need of love;
And feeling still,
with a grief half glad,
That the bad are as good
as the good are bad,
He strikes straight out
for the right-and he
Is the kind of man
for you and me.

JAMES WHITCOMB RILEY.

Some folks are always
puntual in being late.

I'm a great believer in luck,
and I find that the harder I
work, the more of it I have!

CHARLES WEST

Prayer must mean something
to us if it is to mean
anything to God.

ARE YOU THANKFUL ENOUGH?

God gave you a gift of 86,400 seconds today. Have you used one to say "thank you?"
WILLIAM A. WARD

The Pilgrims made seven times more graves than huts. No Americans have been more impoverished than these who, nevertheless, set aside a day of thanksgiving.
H.U. WESTERMAYER

Silent gratitude isn't much use to anyone.
G.B. STERN

If the only prayer you said in your whole life was, "thank you," that would suffice.
MEISTER ECKHART

There is no such thing as gratitude unexpressed. If it is unexpressed, it is plain, old-fashioned ingratitude.
ROBERT BRAULT

Gratitude is the memory of the heart.
JEAN BAPTISTE MASSIEU

When we were children we were grateful to those who filled our stockings at Christmas time. Why are we not grateful to God for filling our stockings with legs?
G.K. CHESTERTON

The only people with whom you should try to get even are those who have helped you.
JOHN E. SOUTHARD

Compassion

A beggar in the street I saw,
Who held a hand like withered claw,
As cold as clay;
But as I had no silver groat
To give, I buttoned up my coat
And turned away.

And then I watched a working wife
Who bore the bitter load of life
With lagging limb;
A penny from her purse she took,
And with sweet pity in her look
Gave it to him.

Anon I spied a shabby dame
Who fed six sparrows as they came
In famished flight;
She was so poor and frail and old,
Yet crumbs of her last crust she doled
With pure delight.

Then sudden in my heart was born
For my sleek self a savage scorn,--
Urge to atone;
So when a starving cur I saw
I bandaged up its bleeding paw
And bought a bone.

For God knows it is good to give;
We may not have so long to live,
So if we can,
Let's do each day a kindly deed,
And stretch a hand to those in need,
Bird, beast or man.

ROBERT SERVICE

You tell me I am getting old

You tell me I am getting old.
I tell you that's not so
The "house" I live in is worn out, and that, of course, I know.
It's been in use a long, long while; it's weathered many a gale.
I'm really not surprised you think it's getting somewhat frail.

The color's changing on the roof, the windows getting dim,
The walls a bit transparent and looking rather thin,
 The foundation's not so steady as once it used to be—
My "house" is getting shaky, but my "house" isn't ME!

My few short years can't make me old. I feel I'm in my youth.
Eternity lies just ahead, a life of joy and truth.
I'm going to live forever, there; Life will go on --it's grand!
You tell me I am getting old? You just don't understand.

The dweller in my little "house" is young and bright and gay!
Just starting on a life to last throughout eternal day
You only see the outside, which is all that most folks see.
You tell me I am getting old?
You've mixed my "house" with ME!

DORA JOHNSON

A couple drove down a country road for several miles, not saying a word. An earlier discussion had led to an argument and neither of them wanted to concede their position.

As they passed a barnyard of mules, goats and pigs, the husband asked sarcastically, "Relatives of yours?"
"Yep," the wife replied, "in-laws."

203

Do not let your fire go out, spark by irreplaceable spark in the hopeless swaps of the not-quite, the not-yet, and the not-at-all. Do not let the hero in your soul perish in lonely frustration for the life you deserved and have never been able to reach. The world you desire can be won. It exists.. it is real.. it is possible.. it's yours.

AYN RAND

Chopsticks

A woman who had worked all her life to bring about good was granted one wish: "Before I die let me visit both hell and heaven." Her wish was granted.

She was whisked off to a great banqueting hall. The tables were piled high with delicious food and drink. Around the tables sat miserable, starving people as wretched as could be. "Why are they like this?" she asked the angel who accompanied her. "Look at their arms," the angel replied. She looked and saw that attached to the people's arms were long chopsticks secured above the elbow. Unable to bend their elbows, the people aimed the chopsticks at the food, missed every time and sat hungry, frustrated and miserable. "Indeed this is hell! Take me away from here!"

She was then whisked off to heaven. Again she found herself in a great banqueting hall with tables piled high. Around the tables sat people laughing, contented, joyful. "No chopsticks I suppose," she said. "Oh yes there are. Look - just as in hell they are long and attached above the elbow but look... here people have learnt to feed one another".

SOMETIME, SOMEWHERE

Unanswered yet? The prayer your lips have pleaded
In agony of heart these many years?
Does faith begin to fail? Is hope departing?
And think you all in vain those falling tears?
Say not the Father hath not heard your prayer;
You shall have your desire, sometime, somewhere.

Unanswered yet? Though when you first presented
This one petition at the Father's throne,
It seemed you could not wait the time of asking,
So urgent was your heart to make it known.
Though years have passed since then, do not despair;
The Lord will answer you sometime, somewhere.

Unanswered yet? Nay, do not say ungranted,
Perhaps your part is not wholly done;
The work began when your first prayer was uttered,
And God will finish what He has begun.
If you will keep the incense burning there,
His glory you shall see, sometime, somewhere.

Unanswered yet? Faith cannot be unanswered;
Her feet are firmly planted on the rock.
Amid the wildest storms she stands undaunted,
Nor quails before the loudest thunder shock.
She knows Omnipotence hath heard her prayer,
And cries, "It shall be done, sometime, somewhere."

OPHELIA G. BROWNING

The Washerwoman's Song

In a very humble cot,
In a rather quiet spot,
In the suds and in the soap,
Worked a woman full of hope;
Working, singing, all alone,
In a sort of undertone:
"With the Savior for a friend,
He will keep me to the end."

Sometimes happening along,
I had heard the semi-song,
And I often used to smile,
More in sympathy than guile;
But I never said a word
In regard to what I heard,
As she sang about her friend
Who would keep her to the end.

Not in sorrow nor in glee
Working all day long was she,
As her children, three or four,
Played around her on the floor;
But in monotones the song
She was humming all day long:
"With the Savior for a friend,
He will keep me to the end."

It's a song I do not sing,
For I scarce believe a thing
Of the stories that are told
Of the miracles of old;

But I know that her belief
Is the anodyne of grief,
And will always be a friend
That will keep her to the end.

Just a trifle lonesome she,
Just as poor as poor could be;
But her spirits always rose,
Like the bubbles in the clothes,
And, though widowed and alone,
Cheered her with monotone,
Of a Savior and a friend
Who would keep her to the end.

I have seen her rub and scrub,
On the washboard in the tub,
While the baby, sopped in suds,
Rolled and tumbled in the duds;
Or was paddling pools,
With old scissors stuck in spools;
She still humming of her friend
Who would keep her to the end.

Human hopes and human creeds
Have their roots in human needs;
And I should not wish to strip
From that washerwoman's lip
Any song that she can sing,
Any hope that song can bring;
For the woman has a friend
Who will keep her to the end.

EUGENE FITCH WARE

211

A woman marries a man expecting he will change, but he doesn't. A man marries a woman expecting that she won't change, and she does.

Why is it harder to lose weight as you get older? Because by that time your body and your fat have become really good friends.

I read some article which said that the symptoms of stress are impulse buying, eating too much and driving too fast. Are they kidding? That's what I call a perfect day.

Why did we put a man on the moon before we realized it would be a good idea to make luggage with wheels?

Why do we say we slept like a baby when they wake up every two hours?

Why do we pay to get to the top of tall buildings, then pay to use binoculars to look at things on the ground?

Married men should forget their mistakes. There is no need for two people to remember the same thing.

A Receipt For Happiness

BEGIN the day with smiling eyes ;
Pursue the day with smiling lips;
Through clouds
perceive the smiling skies
Up where the smiling
sunbeam trips.

Let smiling thoughts
within your mind
Drive gloom
and cold despair apart,
And promptings of a genial kind
Keep ever growing in your heart.

Meet trouble with a cheery mien,
Be jovial in the face of care
He routs all mischief
from the scene
Who greets it with a jocund air.
JOHN K BANGS

AS WE PRAY

Only, o Lord, in Thy dear love
Fit us for perfect rest above;
And help us this and every day.
To live more nearly as we pray
JOHN KEBLE

The World Is Mine

Upon a bus today, I saw a lovely maiden with golden hair. I envied her, she seemed so gay, and wished that I were as fair.
When suddenly she arose to leave, she hobbled down the aisle.
She had one foot and she wore a crutch, but when she passed, a Smile.

Oh God, forgive me when I whine:
I have two good feet, the world is mine.
I stopped to buy some sweets:
the youth who sold them had such charm.
I visited with him, and he said,
"It's so nice to talk with folk like you.
I, as you can see, am blind.
Oh God, forgive me when I whine:
I have two good eyes, the whole world is mine.

In walking down the street, I saw a lad with eyes of blue. He stood while others played, and seemed to know not what to do.
I paused a moment, and said, "Why don't you play with the others dear?"
He said not a word, but looked straight ahead, and then I know he could not hear.

Oh God, forgive me when I whine:
I have two good ears, the world is mine.
With feet to take me where I'd go,
With eyes to see the sunset glow,
With ears to hear what I would know –
Oh God, forgive me when I whine:
I am blessed indeed, the world is mine.

Some things don't last forever, but some things do. Like a good song, or a good book, or a good memory you can take out and unfold in your darkest times, pressing down on the corners and peering in close, hoping you still recognize the person you see there.

SARAH DESSEN

Barbara Walters, of Television's 20/20, did a story on gender roles in Kabul, Afghanistan several years before the Afghan conflict. She noted that women customarily walked five paces behind their husbands.

She recently returned to Kabul and observed that women still walk behind their husbands. From Ms.Walters' vantage point, despite the overthrow of the oppressive Taliban regime, the women now seem to walk even further back behind their husbands, and are happy to maintain the old custom.

Ms. Walters approached one of the Afghani women and asked, 'Why do you now seem happy with an old custom that you once tried so desperately to change?'

The woman looked Miss Walters straight in the eyes, and without hesitation said, 'Land Mines.'

Moral of the story is (no matter what language you speak and where you go):

BEHIND EVERY MAN, THERE'S A SMART WOMAN

Hatred paralyzes life; love releases it. Hatred confuses life; love harmonizes it. Hatred darkens life; love illumines it.

MARTIN LUTHER KING, JR.

Laugh and be merry, remember, better the world with a song,

Better the world with a blow in the teeth of a wrong.
Laugh, for the time is brief, a thread the length of a span.
Laugh and be proud to belong to the old proud pageant of man.

Laugh and be merry: remember, in olden time.
God made Heaven and Earth for joy He took in a rhyme,
Made them, and filled them full with the strong red wine of His mirth
The splendid joy of the stars: the joy of the earth.

So we must laugh and drink from the deep blue cup of the sky,
Join the jubilant song of the great stars sweeping by,
Laugh, and battle, and work, and drink of the wine outpoured
In the dear green earth, the sign of the joy of the Lord.

Laugh and be merry together, like brothers akin,
Guesting awhile in the rooms of a beautiful inn,
Glad till the dancing stops, and the lilt of the music ends.
Laugh till the game is played; and be you merry, my friends.

JOHN MASEFIELD

A one dollar bill met a twenty dollar bill and said, "Hey, where've you been? I haven't seen you around here much."

The twenty answered, "I've been hanging out at the casinos, went on a cruise and did the rounds of the ship, back to the United States for a while, went to a couple of baseball games, to the mall, that kind of stuff. How about you?"

The one dollar bill said, "You know, same old stuff ... church, church, church."

Don't ever forget

Your presence is a gift to the world,
You're unique and one of a kind.
Your life can be what you want it to be.
Take it one day at a time.
Count your blessings, not your troubles,
And you'll make it through what comes along.
Within you are so many answers.
Understand, have courage, be strong.
Don't put limits on yourself.
Your dreams are waiting to be realized.
Don't leave your important decisions to chance.
Reach for your peak, your goal, and your prize.
Nothing wastes more energy than worrying.
The longer a problem is carried, the heavier it gets.
Don't take things too seriously.
Live a life of serenity, not a life of regrets.
Remember that a little love goes a long way.
Remember that a lot goes forever.
Remember that friendship is a wise investment,
Life's treasures are people... together.
Have health and hope and happiness.
And don't ever forget for even a day...
How very special YOU are!
God has created you for a purpose.
You did not come from apes.
You are wonderfully and beautifully made.
Make sure you make a difference
where you are and you do it today.

Thank You

There is an African proverb that states that it takes a whole village to raise a child. A book is no different. It is the combined, assiduous effort of many people to put an idea to form. Many people helped me in this new book, and I hope I have remembered you all, but if by human error, you find yourself not listed here, do remember that you are in my heart.

My heartfelt thanks to:

Mumma, my mother for always inspiring me.

Rishi, my son and my daughter Minakshi for many hours of typing.

Mona Thakkar, my sister for her insights in this project.

Bansari, who motivated me, and helped type & edit its content.

Frenny Diaz, my fantastic (or should I say frentastic) layout artist.

George, for believing in the book and all his help in putting it out in hands of others.

Daniel Pyo, for all his help in making this book happen,

Prerna, in Bombay who believed in the the first one so much,

My friends and customers at Silver World who supported it,

Autumn Bruno for her sincere wishes

Barbara Lee, Ms. Bernardine, & Debra for sharing so many copies with their friends and family.

Diane Downey for sharing memories of her mother Edna Downey, and I would like to thank you, dear reader for your support.

It was my good fortune to have met many individuals who motivated me and helped me grow and believe in the goodness and grandness of life. I read their books, listened to their wise talks, and now I share them with you in this and my other books. They were kind enough to allow me to reprint their writings for the benefit of all mankind.

GARTHS HENRICH OF LITCHFIELD, Illinois was a good friend who was an avid supporter of my earlier projects, especially the magazine that I ran in the early eighties, called Words of Wisdom. He said, One does not find friends, one recognizes them.

WILLIAM ARTHUR WARD (1921-1994), or Uncle Bill, as I called him wrote to me while I was still in India and inspired me with his wise sayings, urging me to follow my goals and dreams. He wrote:
> If you can imagine it, you can achieve it.
> If you can dream it, you can become it.

WILFERD ARLAN PETERSON (1900 - 1995), was a truly genuine person. He wrote The Art of Living series of books in the sixties. I would call him the Elbert Hubbard of modern times.

REV. MAURO FERRERO, OR J. MAURUS, as he is well known as, has written for over fifty years on inspiration, motivation and self-help. His books were my first treasure. I still own most of his original books. He urged me to put together my first book. He now lives outside Rome, Italy.

It was my friend Barbara Lee who gifted Ms. Edna a copy of Flowers from my garden Vol. 1 last christmas. One saturday morning in February, Ms Edna called me to tell me how much she had enjoyed the book. She asked me to keep spreading the good messages and that she would be looking forward to the next book. Ms. Edna passed away on March 17th, 2010. I am sure that she is blessing this book from the heavens above. It was a privilege to have known her. I thank her daughter Diane for sharing this picture of her mother with me.

In Loving Memory of
Edna May Downey

Enjoy 224 pages

of inspirational poems, stories & quotations. From ancient to modern writers, this book is a result of over 25 years of reading, and collecting good thoughts on all of life's virtues and blessings.

MAKES A GREAT GIFT!

Something for the whole family...

After the success of the first and second printing, once again we release the first volume of Flowers from my Garden, in a special gift book edition.

Designed with beautiful color photos, this new edition of 224 pages makes a good gift for all occasions. This book will be a sure welcome in all homes and libraries.

Within its pages readers will find inspiration and motivation in prose and poetry, wisdom for daily living and a dose of wit, to help spread good cheer, understanding and tolerance. Truly, this book is "for all the family."

It makes a thoughtful gift for the children, the elderly, for hospital and nursing home libraries, and for your own personal collection. This book has "No Expiry Date". Its messages will always be fresh and needed!

Next time you want to give a birthday gift, or an anniversary present, or just a gift because your heart says so, order a copy of this delightful "feel better book."

To order copies of the book, Flowers From My Garden Vol. 1 send $24.95 (plus $5 postage & handling) to:

Works of Wisdom
406 Jay St. Brooklyn, NY – 11201
Tel: 917-306-3128 Email: yuvanyc@gmail.com

Yuvaraaj Thakkar has been collecting quotes and inspirational stories since his childhood days in Mumbai (then Bombay), India. He was exposed to different genres of books, thanks to his parents, and had many mentors guiding him, both in India and abroad. His library at home holds many rare books from which he draws his inspiration.

His unique way of organizing and compiling poetry, quotations and stories is refreshing. The stories are gripping, the poetry used in the books will make you feel inspired and the anecdotes will bring a smile on your face.

His life has been influenced by these quotes and stories and he has a high regard for people who influence many lives in a positive way.

Compiling books about inspirational thoughts is his way of thanking those people who inspired him and made him bring a positive change in his life. Here is hoping and wishing that this book changes your life in a positive way.

Currently, he is at work on a book based on the major faiths of the world.

He can be reached at yuvanyc@gmail.com, or by telephone at (917) 306-3128.

Every book has a last page, so does this one. As I take your leave, I will share with you, dear reader, this lovely poem on friendship. What a wonderful feeling it is to have good friends, who are our "found" family. Be a friend to those who need and you will never lack one in your needs.

I cannot ease your aching heart,
Nor take your pain away;
But let me stay and take your hand
And walk with you today.

I'll listen when you need to talk,
I'll wipe away your tears;
I'll share your worries when they come,
I'll help you face your fears.

I'm here and I will stand by you,
On each hill you have to climb;
So take my hand, let's face the world
And live just one day at a time.

You're not alone, for I'm still here,
I'll go that extra mile;
And when your grief is easier,
I'll help you learn to smile!

A book is like
a garden carried
in the pocket.
CHINESE PROVERB